Presented to:

Frank + Joya

Presented by:

Mom + Dad

Date:

25 Dec 2001

God's Little Devotional Book
for Parents

Honor Books
Tulsa, Oklahoma

God's Little Devotional Book for Parents
ISBN 1-56292-789-2
Copyright © 2000 by Honor Books
P.O. Box 55388
Tulsa, Oklahoma 74155

Manuscript prepared by Patsy Petree of A. K. Jacobson & Associates.

Introduction

As a parent, you face one of the most challenging and rewarding responsibilities in today's society: raising the next generation. It's a tough, yet rewarding, assignment, and you're not in this alone. With God's help, you can live a life full of joy and promise as you guide your children into adulthood.

God's Little Devotional Book for Parents is filled with short illustrations and stories that will inspire you to draw strength and wisdom from God. These devotionals are linked to relevant passages of Scripture and quotations that cover a wide range of topics. Each provides a message of strength, hope, and encouragement to bring God into your family life. Use this book as a reference to share your understanding with other parents.

As you read the following pages, we believe that you will come to the realization that God's Word contains all the answers for life and is guaranteed to provide insight and inspiration to parents everywhere.

> *Teach a child to trust in God,*
> *not the morning headlines.*

Some teenage girls formed a "do without" club to raise money for missions. They determined to add to their fund by sacrificial giving. The majority of the girls were from well-to-do homes and easily found ways to contribute. Margie was different. Her family had little in the way of extras, and she found it extremely difficult to find something to contribute. One day she knelt by her bed and asked God to show her something she could do without. As she prayed, her pet spaniel licked her hands. Suddenly, she remembered that the family doctor had offered to buy him.

The tears came as she exclaimed, "Oh, Bright, I can't think of parting with you!" Then she thought of God's gift to the world.

"I'll do it!" she said. Going to the doctor's home, she sold the dog for fifty dollars. Even though she missed her pet, she was still happy.

After learning of Margie's reason for selling her dog, the doctor returned him to her with a note attached to Bright's collar. It read: "Last night I offered what's left of my wasted life to God. I'd like to join your club, and begin by doing without Bright."[1]

Trust in the LORD forever,
for the LORD, the LORD, is the Rock eternal.
ISAIAH 26:4

On a recent flight, two small children who were not happy about being on an airplane disrupted everyone else's peace. Their cries and complaints filled the cabin as they climbed all over the seats and ran up and down the aisle. The parents did everything they could to calm the children down, but nothing worked. Finally, they just gave up and let the children run wild. It was obvious from the behavior of the little boy and his sister that they were not used to being disciplined.

There are two great injustices that can befall a child: One is to punish him for something he didn't do. The other is to let him get away with something he knows is wrong.

Just before takeoff, a flight attendant stopped next to them and said with a big smile, "What is all this squawking up here?" After charming the fussy three-year-old and his older sister for a few minutes, the flight attendant bent down and whispered seriously, "I must remind you that this is a non-squawking flight."

The little ones became unbelievably quiet and remained that way during the entire flight, much to the relief of the rest of the passengers.

Your children's behavior affects everyone around them. Teach them to respect others by making every day a non-squawking journey.[2]

The LORD is known by his justice.
PSALMS 9:16

9

> *Stop trying to perfect your child, but keep trying to perfect your relationship with him.*

A crew of botanists was searching in the Alps for rare flowers. A very fine specimen was spotted on a small ledge of rock that could only be reached with a lifeline. The job was far too dangerous for the inexperienced botanists, so they called in a local shepherd boy who was familiar with the region. They offered him several gold coins to climb down the rope and recover the rare flower.

Although the boy desperately wanted the coins, he feared that the task was too risky. Several times he peered over the edge of the cliff, but he couldn't see any safe way of getting to the flower. Besides, he would have to place his belief in the hands of the strangers who would be holding his lifeline.

Then the boy had an idea. He left the group for a few moments and finally returned holding the hand of a much older man. The shepherd boy then ran eagerly to the brink of the cliff and said to the botanists, "You can tie the rope under my arms now. I'll go into the canyon, as long as you let my father hold the rope."

This boy shared a trusting relationship with his father and was willing to put his life into his father's hands.

In the same way that your children trust in you, put your trust in your heavenly Father today.[3]

A cheerful look brings joy to the heart,
and good news gives health to the bones.
PROVERBS 15:30

Al Covino, a high school coach, was officiating a championship basketball game between New Rochelle, coached by Dan O'Brien, and Yonkers High. The roar from the crowd was deafening.

With only thirty seconds left to play, Yonkers led by one point. New Rochelle pushed the ball up court for the final shot. The ball

> *Life affords no greater responsibility, no greater privilege, than the raising of the next generation.*

rolled around the rim and then off. The crowded gym was in pandemonium! New Rochelle recovered the ball and tapped it in for what looked like victory.

Coach Covino looked at the clock and saw that the game was over, but he hadn't heard the final buzzer because of all the noise. He approached the timekeeper for help. The young man replied, "Mr. Covino, the buzzer went off as the ball rolled off the rim and before the final tap-in was made."

Coach Covino went to Coach O'Brien to give him the bad news. "Dan, time ran out before the final tap-in was made."

Just then, the young timekeeper walked over. He said to Coach O'Brien, "Dad, I'm sorry. The time ran out before the final basket."

Coach O'Brien's face lit up. "That's okay, son," he said. "You did what you had to do. I'm proud of you."

This son reflected his father's example of honesty and good sportsmanship. Can your children count on you to be a good sport?[4]

He decreed statutes . . . and established the law . . . which he commanded our forefathers to teach their children, so the next generation would know them.
PSALMS 78:5-6

> *Having children makes one no more a parent than having a piano makes you a pianist.*

There was once a family of children who wanted a hamster as a pet. They talked their mother into getting one as long as they agreed to take care of it. It would be their responsibility to feed and water the hamster, as well as keep the cage clean. Two months later when Mother was having to care for the hamster, she decided to find a new home for it. She broke the news to the children when they returned home from school that afternoon. They took it quite well; however, they did offer some comments.

One of the children said, "He's been around here a long time. We'll miss him."

Mom agreed, saying, "Yes, but he's too much work for one person, and since I'm that one person, I say he goes."

Another child remarked, "Well, maybe if he wouldn't eat so much and wouldn't be so messy, we could keep him."

Mom was firm. "It's time to take Danny to his new home now," she insisted. "Go and get his cage."

With one voice and in tearful outrage, the children shouted, "Danny? We thought you said 'Daddy'!"

When you communicate with your children, make sure you're on the same wavelength![5]

With your right hand you save me.
The Lord will fulfill his purpose for me;
your love, O Lord, endures forever.
PSALMS 138:7-8

Thomas Edison wrote the following tribute to his mother:

"I did not have my mother long, but she cast over me a good influence that lasted all my life. The good effects of her early training I can never lose. If it had not been for her appreciation and her faith in me at a critical time in my experience, I would never likely have become an inventor. I was always a careless boy, and with a mother of different mental caliber, I would have turned out badly. But her firmness, her sweetness, her goodness were potent powers to keep me on the right path. My mother was the making of me. The memory of her will always be a blessing to me."

> *Correction does much, but encouragement does more. Encouragement after censure is as the sun after a shower.*

Parents, reassure your children that you discipline them for the things they do and not for the people they are. Tell them of your love for them and show them how important they are in your eyes. Encourage, praise, and respect their efforts. Make a memory for your children that will be a blessing to them just as Thomas Edison's mother made for him.[6]

Encourage and rebuke with all authority.
TITUS 2:15

> *There is no finer investment for any community than putting milk into babies.*

Raymond Dunn Jr. was born in 1975 in the state of New York. The Associated Press reported that at his birth he suffered a skull fracture and oxygen deprivation that caused severe retardation. The family discovered further impairments as Raymond grew. His twisted body suffered up to twenty seizures per day, and he was blind, mute, and immobile. He had severe allergies that limited him to only one food: a meat-based formula made by Gerber Foods.

Gerber stopped making the formula that Raymond lived on in 1985. His mother searched the country to buy what stores had in stock, amassing cases and cases, but her supply ran out in 1990. In desperation, she appealed to Gerber for help. Raymond would starve to death without this particular food.

The Gerber employees listened. In an unparalleled action, volunteers donated hundreds of hours to bring out old equipment, set up production lines, obtain special approval from the USDA, and produce the formula—all for one special boy.

Raymond, known as the Gerber Boy, died in January 1995 from his physical problems. During his brief lifetime, he called forth a wonderful essence called compassion.[7]

Our Father in heaven. . . .
Give us today our daily bread.
MATTHEW 6:9,11

In the book *Little Women*, Mrs. March tells this story to her daughters:

"Once upon a time, there were four girls who had enough to eat and drink and wear, a good many comforts and pleasures . . . yet they were not contented. . . . These girls made many excellent resolutions; but they . . . were constantly saying, 'If we only had this,' or 'If we could only do that. . . .' So they asked an old woman what spell they could use to make them

> When we set an example of honesty, our children will be honest. When we encircle them with love, they will be loving. . . . When we meet life with laughter and a twinkle in our eye, they will develop a sense of humor.

happy, and she said, 'When you feel discontented, think over your blessings, and be grateful.'

"They decided to try her advice, and soon were surprised to see how well off they were. One discovered that money couldn't keep shame and sorrow out of rich people's houses; another that . . . she was a great deal happier with her youth, health, and good spirits than a certain fretful, feeble old lady, who couldn't enjoy her comforts; a third that, disagreeable as it was to help get dinner, it was harder still to have to go begging for it; and the fourth, that even carnelian rings were not so valuable as good behavior."

Children are more apt to remember what they learn by observation or example. What do your children see in you?[8]

These things happened to them as examples—as object lessons to us—to warn us against doing the same things.
1 CORINTHIANS 10:11 TLB

We must teach our children how to dream with their eyes open.

It Couldn't Be Done

"Somebody said that it couldn't be done, but he with a chuckle replied

That maybe it couldn't, but he would be one who wouldn't say so 'till he tried.'

So he buckled right in with the trace of a grin on his face. If he worried, he hid it.

He started to sing as he tackled the thing that couldn't be done, and he did it.

Somebody scoffed: 'Oh, you'll never do that; at least no one ever has done it.'

But he took off his coat and took off his hat and the first thing he knew he'd begun it. . . .

There are thousands to tell you it cannot be done. There are thousands to prophesy failure;

There are thousands to point out to you, one by one, the dangers that wait to assail you.

But just buckle right in with a bit of a grin, then take off your coat and go to it;

Just start in to sing as you tackle the thing that cannot be done, and you'll do it."[9]

For as he thinketh in his heart, so is he.
PROVERBS 23:7 KJV

Two young brothers, carpenters by trade, owned property jointly. One of these was the old tumbled down place of their birth. One of the two brothers was soon to be married, and the old house was to be torn down to make room for a new one.

As they entered the house and began demolishing the place, floods

> *A child's education should begin at least one hundred years before he is born.*

of tender memories swept over them again and again. By the time they entered the kitchen, they were nearly overcome with their emotions. This was where the old kitchen table had stood with the family Bible on top. It was where they had knelt every evening for prayer. They remembered now with regret how in later years they had felt a little superior to that time-honored custom carefully observed by their father.

One brother said to the other, "We're better off than he was, but we're not better men."

It is important to remember the customs of our past as they relate to our future. Teach your children the history of your family.[10]

Think constantly about these commandments
I am giving you today. You must
teach them to your children and talk
about them when you are at home.
DEUTERONOMY 6:6-7 TLB

> *Imagination is more important than knowledge.*

The 3M Company is unique among many large corporations. To encourage creativity, the company allows its researchers to spend 15 percent of their time on any project that interests them.

Several years ago, Art Fry, a scientist in 3M's commercial office, took advantage of this creative time and came up with an idea for one of 3M's best-selling products. It all started when he vowed to find a solution to a small irritation he faced every Sunday morning. As a member of his church choir, he routinely marked pages in the hymnal with small bits of paper, but the little pieces were always falling out on the floor.

Then Fry had an idea. He remembered an adhesive developed by a coworker that everyone thought was a failure because it did not stick well. "I coated the adhesive on a paper sample," Fry recalls, "and I found that it was not only a good bookmark, but it was great for writing notes. It will stay in place as long as you want it to, and then you can remove it without damage."

The resulting product was called Post-it! It has become one of 3M's most successful office products.

Make a major investment in the creative processes of your child. One day, he or she might invent something to benefit us all.[11]

Direct my footsteps according to your word.
PSALMS 119:133

F. W. Woolworth was a young store clerk when he tried to persuade his boss to have a ten-cent sale to reduce inventory. The boss agreed, and the idea was a resounding success. This inspired Woolworth to open his own store and price items at a nickel and a dime. He needed capital for such a venture,

> *Children are apt to live up to what you believe of them.*

so he asked his boss to invest the capital in return for part interest in the store. His boss turned him down flat. "The idea is too risky," he told Woolworth. "There are not enough items to sell for five and ten cents."

Woolworth went ahead without his boss' help. Not only was he successful in his first store, but he eventually owned a chain of F. W. Woolworth stores across the nation. Later, his former boss was heard to remark, "As far as I can figure out, every word I used to turn Woolworth down cost me about a million dollars."

This young man was not afraid to follow his dream and put his original, innovative ideas into practice. He was willing to make the tough choices and live up to his full potential. What role models he must have had! Someone in his childhood had taught him to believe in himself.[12]

Many . . . have done well,
but you excel them all.
PROVERBS 31:29 NKJV

> *When you put faith, hope,
> and love together, you can raise
> positive kids in a negative world.*

In an interview published in *People Weekly*, gospel singer CeCe Winans talked candidly about raising her children. She had grown up in a Christian home and was not even allowed to wear makeup until she was eighteen, so she wasn't about to embrace pop rock professionally or personally.

"I don't listen to secular music at home," said Winans, who lives in Nashville with her husband and manager, Alvin Love, and their kids, Alvin III and Ashley. "Very seldom do you find a mainstream artist who does only clean music. It's hard for me to wonder whether my children are going to listen to just the clean songs, so it's better to eliminate that music altogether."

CeCe made it clear that parents are responsible for the atmosphere that surrounds their children in the home. She understood her responsibilities and eliminated those things that she felt were detrimental to her children's spiritual growth.

Parents have many difficult decisions to make in the raising of their children. Often that means they have to give up something for themselves to substitute positive influences and reinforce the values of faith, hope, and love in the home.[13]

God did not give us a spirit of cowardice,
but rather a spirit of power and
of love and of self-discipline.
2 TIMOTHY 1:7 NRSV

No Excuse Sunday

- Cots will be placed in the foyer for those who say, "Sunday is my only day to sleep in."

- We have steel helmets for those who say, "The roof would cave in if I ever came to church."

> *Children have more need of models than of critics.*

- Blankets will be furnished for those who think the church is too cold, and fans for those who say it is too hot.

- We have hearing aids for those who say, "The preacher speaks too softly," and cotton balls for those who say, "He preaches too loudly."

- Score cards will be available for those who wish to list the hypocrites present.

- Some relatives will be in attendance for those who like to go visiting on Sundays.

- There will be TV dinners for those who can't go to church and cook dinner also.

- One section will be devoted to trees and grass for those who like to worship God in nature.

- Finally, the sanctuary will be decorated with Christmas poinsettias and Easter lilies for those who have never seen the church without them.

The above selection was taken from a church bulletin. Which of these behaviors are you modeling for your children? We hope none of them![14]

In everything set them an example
by doing what is good.
TITUS 2:7

> *A baby is something you carry inside you for nine months, in your arms for three years, and in your heart till the day you die.*

Cathy Rigby was a member of the U.S. Women's Gymnastics Team in the 1972 Olympics at Munich, and she had only one goal in mind—to win a gold medal. She had trained hard over a long period of time and knew she was ready to compete.

On the day she was scheduled to perform, she prayed for strength and the control to get through her routine without making mistakes. She was tense with determination not to let herself or the American team down.

She performed well, but when it was finished and the winners announced, her name was not among them. Cathy was crushed by her defeat. Afterward she joined her parents in the stands all set for a good cry. As she sat down, she could barely manage to say, "I'm sorry. I did my best."

"You know that, and I know that," her mother said, "and I'm sure God knows that, too." Then Cathy recalls, her mother said ten words that she has never forgotten: "Doing your best is more important than being the best."

Help your kids understand that whether they win or lose, you still love them. In God's eyes, all of His children are winners![15]

Lo, children are an heritage of the LORD.

PSALMS 127:3 KJV

In an article in *Focus on the Family* magazine, one father described a Thanksgiving that he would never forget. During a family gathering, an older cousin introduced his innocent seventh-grade son to contemporary Christian music.

Overnight his son wasn't satisfied with the children's tunes he'd grown up with and sang in church. The music had to

> *Govern a family as you would cook a small fish—very gently.*

be more loud, rhythmic, and intense. The man and his wife were upset that this cousin had dragged their son away from the "refined" musical taste they had carefully instilled.

It took a week of late-night debate between husband and wife before they finally admitted that their son was growing up. He had stumbled into one of the issues that almost all teenagers use to exhibit their individuality and rattle their parents' cages. The parents reluctantly decided to judge their son's songs by the lyrics rather than the beat. As the teenage years went along, music turned out to be a blessing in their home rather than a source of anxiety.

Allow your child the freedom to grow in ways that may not be the same as yours.[16]

*Peacemakers who sow in peace
raise a harvest of righteousness.*
JAMES 3:18

> *A family is a place where principles are hammered and honed on the anvil of everyday living.*

Families grow strong only when parents invest precious time in their children. In *New Man* magazine, Gary Oliver writes about a difficult decision made by professional baseball player Tim Burke:

While working as a successful pitcher for the Montreal Expos, Tim and his wife wanted to start a family, but discovered they were unable to have children. After much prayer, they decided to adopt four special-needs children. This led to one of the most difficult decisions of Tim's life.

The successful baseball player discovered that his life on the road conflicted with his ability to be a quality husband and father. Over time, it became clear that he couldn't do a good job at both. After much prayer and soul-searching, Tim made what many considered an unbelievable decision: he decided to give up professional baseball.

When Tim left the stadium for the last time, reporters wanted to know why he was retiring. "Baseball is going to do just fine without me," he said. "It's not going to miss a beat. But I'm the only father my children have. I'm the only husband my wife has. And they need me a lot more than baseball does."

It's important to be available to your children to help them make the little everyday decisions of life. Then as they grow up, you can have confidence about how they'll handle the bigger ones.[17]

And David shepherded them with integrity of heart; with skillful hands he led them.
PSALMS 78:72

Henry Ward Beecher was considered by many to be one of the most effective and powerful pulpit orators in the history of the United States. He had a reputation for having a sensitive heart and a great love of the sea. Many of his sermons contained loving anecdotes with a seafaring flavor.

> *Children are the hands by which we take hold of heaven.*

Beecher once said, "Children are the hands by which we take hold of heaven." He had the following to say about a mother's relationship with her child: "A babe is a mother's anchor. She cannot swing far from her moorings. And yet a true mother never lives so little in the present as when by the side of the cradle. Her thoughts follow the imagined future of her child. That babe is the boldest of pilots, and guides her fearless thoughts down through scenes of coming years. The old ark never made such voyages as the cradle daily makes."

What a wonderful image to think of a child as being on a voyage from heaven through life to return to heaven's port one day! It is a tremendous challenge and responsibility to educate, prepare, and assist your children as they continue on that voyage. You have an extraordinary opportunity to join them in their journey.[18]

Because the Lord is my Shepherd,
I have everything I need!
PSALMS 23:1 TLB

To bring up a child in the way he should go, travel that way yourself once in a while.

Jimmy and his father were fishing early one evening on a lake in upstate New York. It was the day before bass season opened, so they were using worms to catch perch and sunfish. Jimmy decided to practice casting with a small silver lure. The minute the lure hit the water, his pole bent double. Jimmy and his dad knew right away that he had something enormous on the line. A giant moon had risen over the lake by the time he reeled in the biggest fish he had ever seen. There was only one problem—it was a bass!

Jimmy's dad looked at his watch and saw that it was 10 p.m., two hours before bass season opened.

"You'll have to put it back, son," he said.

Jimmy protested, "There'll never be another fish as big as this one!"

He looked around and saw no one else on the water to observe the situation. But he knew by the tone of his father's voice that there would be no discussion. He carefully worked the hook from the bass and lowered it gently back into the water.

Jimmy was right. He has never again seen a bass that big. But he does remember the lesson his dad taught him that night. Doing right doesn't mean just when someone is watching![19]

Love the LORD your God with all your heart and with all your soul and with all your strength. These commandments that I give you today are to be upon your hearts. Impress them on your children.
DEUTERONOMY 6:5-7

A man noticed a woman in the grocery store with a three-year-old girl in her basket. As they passed the cookie section, the little girl asked for cookies and her mother told her no. The little girl started to whine and fuss, and the mother said quietly, "Now, Monica, don't be upset. We just have half the aisles left to go through. It won't be long."

> *Reasoning with a child is fine, if you can reach the child's reason without destroying your own.*

Soon they came to the candy aisle, where the little girl began to shout for candy. When told she couldn't have any, she began to scream. The mother said, "There, there, Monica, don't cry—only two more aisles to go, and then we'll be checking out."

When they got to the checkout stand, the little girl immediately clamored for gum. She burst into a terrible tantrum upon discovering there'd be no gum purchased. The mother patiently said, "Monica, we'll be through this checkout stand in five minutes and then you can go home and have a nice nap."

The man followed them out to the parking lot and stopped the woman to commend her. "I couldn't help noticing how patient you were with little Monica," he said.

At that time the mother said, "I'm Monica. My little girl's name is Tammy."

Sometimes the only way to make it through the day is to talk yourself through it![20]

A good man's speech reveals
the rich treasures within him.
MATTHEW 12:35 TLB

45

> ## *Love is a gift from God.*

Karl Menninger once said, "Love cures people—both the ones who give it and the ones who receive it." He organized the work of the Menninger Clinic around love. "From the top psychiatrist down to the electricians and caregivers," Menninger said, "all contacts with patients must manifest love." And it was "love unlimited." The result was that hospitalization time was cut in half.

One of the patients at the clinic was a woman who sat in her rocking chair for three years and never said a word to anyone. Her doctor called a nurse and said, "Mary, I'm giving you Mrs. Brown as your patient. All I'm asking you to do is to love her till she gets well." The nurse tried it. She got a rocking chair of the same kind as Mrs. Brown's, sat beside her, and loved her morning, noon, and night. On the third day, Mrs. Brown spoke. Within a week, she was out of her shell—and well.

Research projects have been done to ascertain the bonding that develops between a mother and her child in the first months after childbirth. Studies have shown that babies deprived of touch and their mothers' voices develop at a slower rate than those held and spoken to. God did not mean for us to grow up in a vacuum. Hug the members of your family daily—both children and adults. We all need love![21]

What a man desires is unfailing love.
PROVERBS 19:22

A ten-year-old boy decided to study judo despite the fact that he had lost his left arm in a devastating car accident. He began lessons with an old Japanese judo master. The boy couldn't understand why the master had taught him only one move.

> Success consists of getting up more times than you fall.

"*Sensei*," the boy finally said, "shouldn't I be learning more moves?"

"This is the only move you know, but this is the only move you'll ever need to know," the *sensei* replied.

Several months later, the boy went to his first tournament. He deftly used his one move to win the first three matches and was now in the finals.

This time his opponent was more experienced. However, the other boy made a critical mistake: He dropped his guard. Instantly, the boy used his move to pin him. The boy had won the match and the tournament.

On the way home, the little boy asked, *"Sensei,* how did I win the tournament with only one move?"

"You won for two reasons," the *sensei* answered. "First, you've almost mastered one of the most difficult throws in all of judo. Second, the only known defense for that move is for your opponent to grip your left arm."

Are you teaching your children the skills they'll need to succeed in life?[22]

For when the way is rough, your patience has a chance to grow. So let it grow, and don't try to squirm out of your problems.
JAMES 1:3-4 TLB

> _Lost time is never_
> _found again._

The two boys were dressed and ready to go. Excitement flooded their faces and all their talk was about only one thing: Their father had promised to take them to the circus that afternoon!

Dad came home from work after lunch and quickly changed into casual clothing. Just as the three of them were about to leave the house, the phone rang. The boys listened as their father talked with the person on the other end of the line. Bit by bit, their faces began to fall. This was obviously a business call. Disappointment rolled into the room like a dark cloud. Their mother also overheard what she thought was the inevitable change of plans. Then to everyone's surprise, they heard Dad say,

"No, I won't be down. It will just have to wait until morning."

He hung up the phone and called for the boys to meet him at the car. As he turned to kiss his wife goodbye, she smiled, and with a tinge of fear that he may have made the wrong decision, she said, "The circus keeps coming back, you know."

Her husband replied, "Yes, I know, but childhood doesn't."

Time goes so quickly. Enjoy your children today.[23]

Children are a gift from God:
they are his reward.
PSALMS 127:3 TLB

As Pam stood in front of the mirror while applying her makeup, she verbally criticized her physical characteristics. From head to toe, she complained about the way she was put together. She desperately wanted her husband's attention so he could rescue her from her lack of self-confidence!

> *If a child lives with approval, he learns to live with himself.*

Bill was lying on the bed appreciating her beauty when Pam began her personal assessment. Rather than ignore her self-criticism, he got up and wrapped his arms around her, giving her a reassuring hug.

Then he stepped back, took her face in his hands, and said, "Pam, let me be your mirror. You are gorgeous! Let me reflect back to you the beautiful woman God has created you to be. If we have to throw all the mirrors in the house away, we will! From now on, I will be your mirror!"

Many lack self-esteem because they were criticized or belittled as children. If you battle with feelings of inferiority, learn to accept yourself for who you are and pass on that gift to your children. God loves you just the way you are![24]

Therefore, accept one another, just as Christ also accepted us to the glory of God.
ROMANS 15:7 NASB

53

> Let your children go if
> you want to keep them.

Bill Cosby writes in *Fatherhood,* "Some authority on parenting once said, 'Hold them very close and then let them go.'" This is the hardest truth for parents to learn: that their children are continually growing away from them. It is, however, a part of the evolution of life. Your children grow to adulthood, establish homes of their own, have your grandchildren, and the cycle of life continues.

Mr. Cosby went on to tell this story about his daughter: "You have to remember that rejection, like one I received on a certain day when I called my daughter at college, means no lessening of her love. Someone in her dorm picked up the phone and I asked to speak to my daughter. The person left and returned about a minute later to say, 'She says she's sleeping right now.'"

A child's rejection hurts, but it doesn't mean that your child loves you any less. Be glad that you have done a good job in preparing him or her to be independent. Use the first rejection to prepare yourself for the many more to come. It's just another stage in their growth and development . . . as well as yours![25]

"So there is hope for your future,"
declares the LORD. "Your children
will return to their own land."
JEREMIAH 31:17

"We were going over multiplication tables in Mrs. Tacy's fourth grade class," John Maxwell remembers in *Focus on the Family* magazine, "when I looked up and saw my dad walk into the classroom.

"'Mrs. Tacy,' I heard my dad say, 'I'm going out of town tomorrow, and I'm

> *What children hear at home soon flies abroad.*

going to take John with me for a few days and teach him.' I couldn't believe it. I was going to get to miss school and spend time with Dad! I about jumped out of my chair.

"Dad continued, 'You've been doing a real good job teaching him, but it's my turn for a while.' Then he turned to me and said, 'I'll see you at home tonight, John.'

"What I remember most about that trip in Dad's Ford Fairlane was talking for hours about everything: baseball, basketball, current events, music, church, school, and my friends. It was the first time I had Dad all to myself.

"That trip with my dad when I was ten really made me feel important and grown up. It also set the tone for how he took charge of my education. He and my mom recognized that they were my most important teachers."

Plan a day to make a special memory for your child.[26]

A wise man's heart guides his mouth,
and his lips promote instruction.
PROVERBS 16:23

> *Children possess an uncanny ability to cut to the core of the issue. . . . They have not acquired the obstructions to faith that come with education.*

A minister was making an appeal for funds one night at a church service. He invited the congregation to bring their gifts and lay them on the altar. The response was huge, and soon the aisles were filled with people bringing up their offerings.

A little girl came slowly toward the front. She was crippled and walked with a crutch. At the altar, she pulled a little ring from her finger and laid it with the other gifts. Adjusting her crutch, she went back to her seat. After the meeting, the preacher said to her, "My dear, I saw your gift tonight. It was beautiful. But, you know, the response of the people tonight has been plentiful, and we find we have some money left over. So we don't need your ring, and I have brought it back to you."

The little girl looked up with rebuke in her eyes, and said, "I didn't give that ring to you. I gave it to the Lord."

Jesus said that the kingdom of heaven belongs to the children. Those who have been taught properly have as much desire to give to God as do adults.[27]

Let the little children come to me, and do not stop them; for it is to such as these that the kingdom of heaven belongs.
MATTHEW 19:14 NRSV

A mother and father helped their oldest son pack his belongings and prepare for his first year of college. The parents had provided their son with every conceivable item that he might need to begin living independently. They also gave him his first checkbook with the funds deposited into the account to pay his beginning college expenses. Two months later, bank overdrafts on the son's account began arriving at the parents' home.

> *You can lead a boy to college, but you cannot make him think.*

"How are things at school?" Dad asked in a phone call to his son.

"Just great, Dad," his son replied.

"John," his dad responded, "you've written over $500 in checks when there was only $10 left in your checking account. You are extensively overdrawn."

· "But that can't be," argued John, "I still have several checks left in my checkbook."

Parents often assume that their children have learned a necessary skill at school, when the reality is, they haven't. They may have been exposed to the information at some point but did not receive any real-life practice to make it a part of their knowledge. Make it a point to teach your children how to balance a checkbook, do the laundry, and comparison shop for groceries. They'll thank you for it later![28]

The hand of the diligent makes rich.
PROVERBS 10:4 NKJV

> *For many little girls, life with father is a dress rehearsal for love and marriage.*

In *Discipleship Journal,* Paul Thigpen wrote of coming home one afternoon to discover that the kitchen he had worked so hard to clean only a few hours before was now a terrible wreck. Obviously, his young daughter had been busy cooking. Ingredients, dirty bowls, and utensils were scattered across the counters and floor. He was not happy.

As he looked a little more closely at the mess, he spied a tiny note on the table, clumsily written and smeared with chocolate fingerprints. The message was short: "I'm makin sumthin 4 you, Dad." It was signed, "Your Angel."

In the midst of all that mess and despite his irritation, joy sprang into his heart. His attention had been redirected from the problem to the little girl he loved. As he encountered her in that brief note that brought her simple goodness into focus, he could take pleasure in seeing her hand at work in a situation that seemed disastrous.

A father is important in a daughter's life. Her self-esteem, ideas on the meaning of love, and knowledge of the importance of marriage all stem from the relationship she has with him.

So the next time you feel tempted to yell at your daughter about her messy room, take a deep breath. Maybe there's a better way to teach her self-discipline.[29]

A happy heart makes the face cheerful,
but heartache crushes the spirit.
PROVERBS 15:13

Many years ago, a man named David received a new car as a gift from his prosperous brother. One evening as Dave was leaving work, he noticed a poor child eyeing his shiny new car.

"Is this your car?" the boy asked.

Dave nodded and said, "My brother gave it to me for Christmas.

> *Allow children to be happy their own way; for what better way will they ever find?*

The boy said, "It didn't cost you anything? Boy, I wish. . . ." David expected the boy to wish that he had a generous brother, but what the boy said astonished Dave. He said, "I wish I could be a brother like that." He asked the young boy if he'd like a ride home. The little boy hopped in quickly.

David smiled, thinking that the boy was anxious to show off to his neighbors and family. Again he was wrong. When the two pulled up in front of the boy's house, the boy asked David to wait a minute. He then ran up the steps and soon returned carrying his crippled brother. Dave was moved deeply when he heard him say, "There it is, Buddy, just like I told you upstairs. His brother gave it to him. Someday I'm gonna give you one just like it." This child found his happiness in the joy of giving. Where could one find a better place to look?[30]

Do not put out the Spirit's fire.
1 THESSALONIANS 5:19

The more a child becomes aware of a father's willingness to listen, the more a father will begin to hear.

A mother and her children went looking for a Father's Day card. Suddenly the youngest child shouted with glee, "I found it! I found it!"

After each of the children had read the card, they passed it to Mom with a unanimous vote and a laugh: "This is it, Mom! This is for Dad."

Mom took the card and saw that it had been written with a small child's block printing. On the front of the card was a little boy with dirty sneakers and untied shoestrings. His cap was twisted to one side, and his jeans were torn. He obviously was dirty and sweaty from playing hard outside, and he was holding onto the handle

GOD'S LITTLE DEVOTIONAL BOOK FOR PARENTS

of a little wagon loaded with broken toys and a baseball bat. In his hip pocket was a slingshot. His eye was black from running into something, and he had a Band-Aid stuck on his arm. The front of the card read: "Dad, I'll never forget that little prayer you said for me every day." And then on the inside of the card were these words: "'God help you if you ever do that again!'"

Sometimes our children can scare us with their foolhardy antics or when they take unnecessary risks. But we need to remember not to overreact like this father did. Discipline your children with love and respect, remembering that you were a kid once, too.[31]

Take note of this: Everyone should be quick to listen, slow to speak and slow to become angry.
JAMES 1:19

A young girl remembers her grandpa as an old man confined to his chair most of the time due to severe arthritis. His Bible always seemed to be cradled on his frail legs.

One time everyone was in the kitchen except the little girl and Grandpa. Grandpa's lunch was brought to him on a tray because it was too difficult for him to eat at the table. The little girl's mother called for her to come and eat. She started to obey, but something made her stop. There sat Grandpa all alone. Her heart was moved with compassion. She went to Grandpa's chair, put her arms around him, and said, "I love you, Grandpa."

Then her grandpa did something she neither expected nor understood at the

When you find a spark of grace in a young heart, kneel down and blow it into a flame.

time: He cried. That small act of kindness meant the world to him.

Regardless of age, we all need a human touch. It creates a connection with others so that we don't feel so alone. We never know how much our random acts of kindness mean to others. Give someone an unexpected hug today![32]

The unfolding of your words gives light;
it gives understanding to the simple.
PSALMS 119:130

When families fail, society fails.

Each morning, the mother walked her frightened kindergartner to her classroom. They faced the same routine every day, going through the same reassuring gestures. The mother wasn't alone in this ritual. In the beginning, there were many teary-eyed children, but they soon grew braver until the group was reduced to two: Sarah and a little boy named Danny.

Danny was brought to class by his father, a man with a square jaw, designer suits, and a perfect smile that would cut through any heart in a flash. Sarah's mother found herself walking with him to their cars every day. From the beginning, she was aware of his attentiveness toward her. He was likable, handsome, and wooing.

70

She began to feel uneasy, but persuaded herself they were not doing anything wrong. Each time they spoke, her feelings of guilt weakened. She enjoyed his friendship, the new attention, and the secret feelings. She told herself again and again, "This is only a friendship."

Then one morning she realized she enjoyed his attention far too much for this to remain a safe place. She changed the time she brought Sarah to school and thanked God for opening her eyes in time.

Keep your family safe by using wisdom when developing relationships with others.[33]

Lord, let our eyes be opened.
MATTHEW 20:33 NRSV

A man who is regarded as a role model for young people today is the great baseball pitcher Orel Hershiser. In his book, *Out of the Blue,* Hershiser describes his own role model as a man who was competitive, yet generous, and a gentleman.

> *Fathering is a marathon, not a sprint.*

"In everything he does," writes Hershiser, "he wants to win. Sometimes he would compete only with himself. I saw that side of him even in how he cleaned the garage. He took care of every detail and put everything in its place."

Hershiser added that his role model always praised and rewarded those who did a good job. He was a perfectionist and often demanded that a job be done over again; but even so, he always gave a pat on the back in encouragement. He didn't mind pain or work. He had a great habit of asking, "Why?" When others might say,

"There goes our golf date tomorrow," because of a rainy forecast, Hershiser's role model would ask instead, "Why? Does the weatherman have to be right? We don't know what tomorrow will be like. The storm may pass through. Let's plan on playing and see if it works out." He was a headstrong optimist, with a never-give-up attitude. Who was Orel Hershiser's role model? His dad!

Do your children look up to you as a role model?[34]

A wise son heeds his father's instruction.
PROVERBS 13:1

> *A father who teaches his children responsibility provides them with a fortune.*

In their book *Cheaper by the Dozen,* Frank B. Gilbreth Jr. and Ernestine Gilbreth Carey described their father as a man who "always practiced what he preached, and it was just about impossible to tell where his scientific management company ended and his family life began. His office was always full of children, and he often took two or three of us, and sometimes all twelve, on business trips. . . . On the other hand, our house at Montclair, New Jersey, was a sort of school for scientific management and the elimination of wasted motions."

Their father placed work charts in the bathrooms, took moving pictures of his children doing chores to help identify wasted motion, and insisted that a child who wanted extra pocket money submit a sealed bid, with the lowest bidder getting the contract. Still, his children didn't seem to mind their regimented life. Why? Primarily because Dad "had a respect for them, too, and didn't mind showing it. It was a love of children more than anything else that made him want a pack of his own."

It's not the rules that a father enacts that cause a child to rebel, but rather, a lack of love and respect.[35]

Listen, my sons, to a father's instruction; pay attention and gain understanding. I give you sound learning, so do not forsake my teaching.
PROVERBS 4:1-2

Most people know of the Great Depression that occurred during the 1930s, but few know about the financial depression in the first half of the 1800s. Governments went into financial panic. Pennsylvania, one of the wealthier states at the time, rejected its debts . . . in effect declaring itself bankrupt. Illinois felt that with such a move made by its wealthy neighbor, it might be justified in doing likewise.

> *Train your child in the way in which you know you should have gone yourself.*

When Stephen Douglas heard of the proposal for bankruptcy, he strongly opposed it. Although ill at the time, he insisted that he be carried to the state legislature on a stretcher. Lying on his back, he made this historic resolution: "That

Illinois be honest." The motion touched the hearts of every member of the state house, and the resolution was adopted with eagerness. The action by Illinois kept the practice of repudiation from spreading among the states. Many historians credit this move as a key reason why Illinois is one of the most prosperous states today.

Choosing the right direction sometimes means choosing the unpopular direction with the greatest amount of discomfort. Teach your children that there is no substitute for the rewards that can come at the end of such a journey.[36]

But blessed is the man who trusts
in the LORD, whose confidence is in him.
JEREMIAH 17:7

> $\mathcal{G}$*ive me the children until they are seven and anyone may have them afterwards.*

The great missionary Dr. Albert Schweitzer tells us in his memoirs that the most important thing his parents did for him when he was a child was to take him to the worship services of their church.

"From the service in which I joined as a child," he wrote, "I have taken with me into life a feeling for what is solemn and a need for quiet and self-recollection without which I cannot realize the meaning of my life. I cannot therefore support the opinion of those who would not let the children take part in grown-up people's services until they to some extent understood them. The important thing is not that they shall understand but that they shall feel something of what is serious and solemn. The

fact that the child sees his parents full of devotion and has to feel something of devotion himself, that is what gives the service its meaning to him."

G. Raymond Campbell also advises parents not to worry about their children's behavior in church. He says that a four-year-old whose parents have a genuine feeling of reverence and worship will be better behaved than some adults who squirm and twist, whisper, and feel no sense of reverence in the presence of God. Children are much more influenced by your behavior than with your words. Model for them your trust in a loving God.[37]

We know and rely on the love
God has for us. God is love. Whoever
lives in love lives in God, and God in him.
1 JOHN 4:16

The following famous prayer, written by Robert Louis Stevenson, embodies what we all desire for our children and extended families. In it, he expresses thanksgiving for even the simplest of life's pleasures and firmly leaves its trials and tribulations at the feet of God:

> *The family is the original Department of Health, Education, and Welfare.*

"Lord, behold our family here assembled. We thank Thee for this place in which we dwell; for the love that unites us; for the peace accorded us this day; for the hope with which we expect the morrow; for the health, the work, the food, and the bright skies that make our lives delightful; for our friends in all parts of the earth, and our friendly helpers in the foreign isle. . . .

"Give us courage, gaiety, and the quiet mind. Spare to us our friends, soften to us our enemies. Bless us, if it may be, in all our innocent endeavors. If it may not, give us the strength to encounter that which is to come, that we be brave in peril, constant in tribulation, temperate in wrath, and in all changes of fortune and down to the gates of death, loyal and loving one to another. Amen."[38]

Finally, brothers, whatever is true, whatever is noble, whatever is right, whatever is pure, whatever is lovely, whatever is admirable—if anything is excellent or praiseworthy—think about such things. . . . Put it into practice. And the God of peace will be with you.
PHILIPPIANS 4:8-9

> *Children have never been good at listening to elders, but they have never failed to imitate them.*

Two little boys were discussing their lives one day, including the various behavioral patterns of their parents. One boy asked, "Does your daddy sit in the den a lot after he comes home from work?"

"No," his friend replied, "he growls all over the place at our house."

Your children not only have a candid opinion of you, but they also are likely to copy your behavior, whether good or bad. Even if your children don't particularly like what you do, they are likely to behave unconsciously in the same way. A two-year-old might walk with a swagger . . . just like Dad. A three-year-old is likely to use all the words his parents use, even the inappropriate ones! Above all, children imitate the way their parents treat one another.

Several little girls were playing house one day, taking turns playing various family members, when one of them said to another, "Now you be the daddy." The little girl thought for a minute and then said, "I don't want to be the daddy. I want to talk, and besides, what would I use for a remote control?"

Children are great imitators! Listen to the echo.[39]

Whatever you do, work at it with all your heart.
COLOSSIANS 3:23

A minister was busy preparing a sermon in his library while his little boy read a picture book by the fireplace nearby. The minister realized that he needed a reference book that he had left upstairs, so he asked his son to get it for him. The little boy was eager to help and quickly ran out of the room.

> *The first duty of love is to listen.*

Several minutes later, the father noticed that his son was taking quite a long time. He got up, walked out of his library, and stopped short at what he saw. His small son was sitting at the top of the staircase crying. The book that the minister wanted lay at the boy's feet.

"Oh, Daddy," the little boy sobbed, "I can't carry it. It's too heavy for me."

In a flash, the father ran up the stairs and scooped both the book and his son into his strong arms and carried them back to the library below.

Often we ask our children to perform tasks that are beyond their capability. We get impatient when their little legs can't keep up with our long strides. Like this wise father, give your child the opportunity to take on responsibility and be ready to lend a helping hand when he or she needs it.[40]

Is there anyone among you who, if your child asks for bread, will give a stone?
MATTHEW 7:9 NSRV

> *There are only two lasting bequests we can hope to give our children. One of these is roots. The other, wings.*

Most important achievements were once considered impossible until someone set the goal to make them a reality.

Lewis Carroll's famous masterpiece, *Through the Looking Glass*, contains a story that exemplifies the need to dream the impossible dream. There is a conversation between Alice and the queen, which goes like this:

"I can't believe that!" said Alice.

"Can't you?" the queen said in a pitying tone. "Try again, draw a long breath, and shut your eyes."

Alice laughed. "There's no use trying," she said. "One can't believe impossible things."

"I dare say you haven't had much practice," said the queen. "When I was your age, I always did it for half an hour a day. Why, sometimes I've believed as many as six impossible things before breakfast."

When you dare to dream, many wonders can be accomplished. Teach your child to dream an impossible dream![41]

Those who hope in the LORD will renew their strength. They will soar on wings like eagles.
ISAIAH 40:31

Thomas J. Watson Jr. writes in *Father, Son & Co.: My Life at IBM and Beyond* about his first few days as CEO: "When my father died in 1956—six weeks after making me head of IBM—I was the most frightened man in America. For ten years he had groomed me to succeed him, and I had been the

> *Kids are not a short-term loan; they are a long-term investment!*

young man in a hurry, eager to take over, cocky, and impatient. Now, suddenly, I had the job. But what I didn't have was Dad there to back me up."

Watson admits that he "didn't have much motivation as a youth." He spent so much time flying airplanes at Brown University that he barely graduated. However, his father continued to encourage him. He said, "At some point, something will catch hold and you are going to be a great man."

Watson returned home after World War II "confident, for the first time that I might be capable of running IBM." During his fifteen years as head of IBM, the company entered the computer era and grew more than tenfold. He says of the success, "I think I was at least successful enough that people could say I was the worthy son of a worthy father."

Continually encourage your children to fulfill God's plan for their lives.[42]

So do not throw away your confidence; it will be richly rewarded. You need to persevere.
HEBREWS 10:35-36

> *What a child is taught*
> *on Sunday, he will*
> *remember on Monday.*

We're a mile and a half from church, you know, and it rains today, so we can't go.

We'd go ten miles to a party or show, though the rains should fall and the winds should blow. That's why, when it rains, we just can't go.

We're a mile and a half from church, you know, and a tire is flat, so we can't go.

We'd fix it twice to make a visit, and if there's a ball game we wouldn't miss it.

We'd mend the tire if at all we could, and if we couldn't, we'd go afoot,

for hunting pleasure is all the style, so the church will have to wait awhile.

90

We're a mile and a half from church, you know, and our friends are coming, so we can't go.

To disappoint our friends would seem unkind, but to neglect worship we don't mind,

if we may please our friends on earth, and spend a day in feasting and mirth.

But, sometime, when we come near the end of our days, we'll go to church and mend our ways.

George C. Degen

Children learn much from the example set by their parents. Remember this poem when your children ask what the family is doing next Sunday.[43]

Apply your mind to instruction and your ear to words of knowledge.
PROVERBS 23:12 NRSV

There was once a little boy who was given everything he wanted. As an infant, he was given a bottle at the first little whimper. He was picked up and held whenever he fussed. His parents said, "He'll think we don't love him if we let him cry."

He was never disciplined for leaving the yard. He suffered no consequences for breaking windows or tearing up flowerbeds. His parents said, "He'll think we don't love him if we stifle his will."

> *The most deprived children are those who have to do nothing in order to get what they want.*

His mother picked up after him and made his bed. His parents said, "He'll think we don't love him if we give him chores."

Nobody ever stopped him from using bad words. He was never reprimanded for scribbling on his bedroom wall. His parents said, "He'll think we don't love him if we stifle his creativity."

He was never required to go to Sunday school. His parents said, "He'll think we don't love him if we force religion down his throat."

One day the parents received news that their son was in jail on a felony charge. They cried to each other, "All we ever did was love and do for him." Unfortunately, that is, indeed, all they did.

Children need boundaries to feel loved. The key is consistency.[44]

Aim for perfection.
2 CORINTHIANS 13:11

*A spoiled child
never loves its mother.*

A local minister was visiting a group home when one small boy decided to test his limits by stomping on the flowerbed. The minister said, "Michael, if you stomp on those flowers one more time, I'm going to spank you."

Michael looked up at him and then looked back down at the flowerbed. Next he raised his foot and smashed the flowers into the ground.

"Okay, come on inside," the minister said. He swatted Michael three times on his bottom, but when he finished, Michael wasn't crying.

"You done?" the little boy asked.

"Yes, but why did you deliberately stomp on those flowers?"

"Because I didn't think you'd spank me."

"Really? Why?"

Michael's answer was in his eyes. They were saying, "No one's loved me enough to discipline me and keep their word."

Sometimes parents are afraid to discipline their children because they fear their children won't love them afterward. But children want you to care. Provide your kids with the order and structure they need to succeed in life.[45]

Discipline your son, and he will give you peace; he will bring delight to your soul.
PROVERBS 29:17

Many times Thomas Edison failed the first or second or tenth time in his attempts to discover something new, but he didn't mind. He just kept on trying! It is said that he made thousands upon thousands of attempts before he got his famous electric light to operate.

> *More depends on my walk than talk.*

One day a workman to whom he had given a task came to him and said, "Mr. Edison, it cannot be done."

"How often have you tried?" asked Edison.

"About two thousand times," replied the man.

"Then go back and try it two thousand more times," said Edison. "You have only found out that there are two thousand ways in which it cannot be done."

This story reveals one of the great truths of life. Keep trying until you get it right!

Sometimes our pessimism or ego or pride or just plain laziness gets in the way of the things we want to accomplish. Think of it in Edison's terminology—you've only found out how many ways it can't be done.

Set a good example for your children by tackling life's roadblocks with a positive attitude.[46]

The fruit of righteousness will be peace;
the effect of righteousness will be
quietness and confidence forever.
ISAIAH 32:17

97

> *Always laugh when you can;*
> *it is cheap medicine.*

On a recent canoe trip to North Carolina, one man was strengthened and lifted up by the childlike joy of a wonderful moment. The following is how he recorded it in his journal:

"Somewhere near the beginning of my river run . . . I heard behind me a joyous tumult of laughter from an oncoming raft . . . I turned just in time to see a large raft filled to overflowing with madly paddling youngsters, all of them in full-throated laughter. It was a raft full of Down's syndrome kids out for a day on the river. Truly uninhibited joy that is rarely seen except in tiny children was erupting in their voices and on their faces. They were feeding upon the moment with such abandon that all else was swept away. Their whole focus, their whole life was right here. Right now. And the power of it was unconquerable, sweeping up everything within the sound of their voices into an all-encompassing joy.

"'Thank you!' I shouted and raised my paddle high in salute to their joy and grace. And wisdom."

Children live in the events of the moment, spontaneously expressing their joy and delight. They don't let thoughts of tomorrow interfere with that joy. Remember to laugh today![47]

For the joy of the LORD is your strength.
NEHEMIAH 8:10

When Columbus presented his plans to discover a new and shorter route to the West Indies, most people in Spain said his plan was impossible. King Ferdinand and Queen Isabella ignored the advice of all the naysayers and financed the voyage. Many believed the world was flat until Columbus, his three ships, and his small group of followers sailed to "impossible" new lands. Columbus said he could make it happen, and he did!

Great hopes make great men.

Many discouraged Henry Ford from pursuing his fledgling idea of a motorcar. However, he remained committed and tirelessly chased his dream. Although his first attempt resulted in a vehicle without a reverse gear, Henry Ford knew he could make it happen.

Orville and Wilbur Wright were ridiculed by people saying, "What a silly and insane way to spend money. Leave flying to the birds." Even their father laughed at the idea of an airplane.

Two more individuals who succeeded at making their ideas come to fruition were Madame Curie and Benjamin Franklin. The experts advised Ms. Curie that her ideas regarding radium were scientifically impossible. Mr. Franklin was admonished to stop his foolish experiments with lightning. Neither stopped their work and both succeeded!

We need the knowledge of the past and the present, combined with the quest for understanding of the future. A child's curiosity can be the beginning of greatness.[48]

*Then he went down to Nazareth with them
and was obedient to them. But his mother
treasured all these things in her heart.
And Jesus grew in wisdom and stature,
and in favor with God and men.*
LUKE 2:51-52

101

> *Love puts the fun
> in together.*

A family planned a vacation to the West Coast one summer. All the plans were made, but at the last minute Dad couldn't go because he had to complete some work that had been delayed. Mom insisted she could do the driving. Dad helped plan their route and made the reservations where they would stop each night.

After two weeks, Dad was able to complete his work and decided to surprise his family. Without calling them, he flew to a city on their route, took a taxi out of the city, and asked to be let out along the highway. According to his travel plan for the family, they would be driving along this same highway later in the day. When he saw the family car, he stuck out his thumb like a hitchhiker. As Mom and the children drove past, one of the children yelled, "Mom, wasn't that Dad!" The car came to a screeching halt, and the family enjoyed a wonderful reunion.

A reporter later asked the father why he did such a crazy thing. He said, "After I die, I want my kids to be able to say, 'Dad sure was fun, wasn't he?'"

Joyful times cause your children to flourish and allow guidance and discipline to seep in.[49]

He will yet fill your mouth with laughter
and your lips with shouts of joy.
JOB 8:21

The great evangelist D. L. Moody was a man of wholesome humor and an occasional practical joke. He sometimes told stories with such enthusiasm that he would laugh until he cried. He enjoyed gathering his associates about him at the close of the day to see who could tell the best stories. When someone asked him how he could laugh so fully after preaching so seriously, he answered, "If I didn't laugh, I would have a nervous breakdown at the pace at which I live."

You grow up the first time you laugh at yourself.

Leslie B. Flynn wrote, "Though people know about the prodigious labors of David Livingstone in opening up Africa for missionary endeavor, few know that in the midst of their lonely life, he and his wife often acted like jolly school kids on an excursion. Mirth saturated their lives so much that Livingstone more than once said to his wife, 'Really, my dear, we ought not to indulge in so many jokes. We are getting too old. It is not becoming. We must be more staid.'"

Appropriate humor is like divine medicine. It cheers the mind, enlightens the message, and relieves the listener.

Give us, Lord,
A bit of sun,
A bit of work,
And a bit of fun.[50]

When a man is gloomy, everything
seems to go wrong; when he is cheerful,
everything seems right!
PROVERBS 15:15 TLB

> *Love is an act of endless forgiveness, a tender look that becomes a habit.*

Andrew Wyermann's favorite Christmas memory took place when he was seven years old. He recalls, "Early Christmas Eve, my mother took my brother and me out for a treat. It was her way to get us out of our fifth-floor apartment in the Bronx while my father prepared for the evening festivity. As we climbed the stairs back to the apartment, the shrill sound of a whistle filled the hallway. Our pace quickened and a second burst of the whistle could be heard. We dashed into the apartment. There was my father, playing engineer with the biggest Lionel train ever made. It was so magnificent, so unexpected, so wonderful!

"Some fifty years later, I still have the train set and cherish it. . . . The train is a warm reminder of the greater gift my parents gave me. Unconditional love was their gift. I never doubted their care for me, and from such grace sprang my own capacity to truth. It was years later that I fully understood the gift my parents gave me had its source in God's gift of the Child to us all. The sound of the whistle and the song of the angels have become one and the same."

Give your children the gift of unconditional love and unexpected laughter. It's an unbeatable combination![51]

So he got up and went to his father.
But while he was still a long way off,
his father saw him and was filled with
compassion for him; he ran to his son,
threw his arms around him and kissed him.
LUKE 15:20

Ten Commandments of Human Relations

1. Speak to people. There is nothing as nice as a cheerful word of greeting.

2. Smile at people. It takes seventy-two muscles to frown, only fourteen to smile.

3. Call people by name. The sweetest music to anyone's ears is the sound of his own name.

> *I talk and talk and talk, and I haven't taught people in fifty years what my father taught by example in one week.*

4. Be friendly and helpful. If you would have friends, be friendly.

5. Be cordial. Speak and act as if everything you do is a genuine pleasure.

6. Be genuinely interested in people. You can like almost anybody if you try.

7. Be generous with praise—cautious with criticism.

8. Be considerate of the feelings of others. There are usually three sides to a controversy: yours, the other fellow's, and the right one.

9. Be alert to give service. What counts in life is what we do for others.

10. Add to this a good sense of humor, a big dose of patience, and a dash of humility, and you will be rewarded manifoldly.

Robert G. Lee penned the above Ten Commandments. Following these precepts will set a wise example. Children learn quickly by imitation.[52]

When words are many, sin is not absent,
but he who holds his tongue is wise.
PROVERBS 10:19

> *The surest way to make it hard for children is to make it easy for them.*

Memos from Your Child

- Don't spoil me. Teach me to share.

- Don't be afraid to be firm with me. I prefer it . . . it makes me feel more secure.

- Don't correct me in front of people if you can help it. I'll take much more notice if you talk to me in private.

- Don't forget the difference between mistakes and sins.

- Don't protect me from consequences. I need to learn the hard way.

- Don't take too much notice of my small ailment. Sometimes they get me the attention I want.

- Don't nag. Give me instruction and guidance.

- Don't make rash promises. Remember that I feel badly let down when promises are broken.

- Don't forget that I cannot explain myself as well as I should like. This is why I'm not always accurate.

- Don't be inconsistent. That completely confuses me and makes me lose my faith in you.[53]

Being punished isn't enjoyable while it is happening—it hurts! But afterwards we can see the result, a quiet growth in grace and character.
HEBREWS 12:11 TLB

One evening in Albany, New York, a man asked a sailor what time it was. The serviceman pulled out a huge watch and replied, "Its 7:20."

The man knew it was later, so he asked, "Your watch has stopped, hasn't it?"

"No," said the sailor, "I'm still on Mountain standard time. I'm from southern Utah. When I joined the navy, Pa gave me this watch. He said it'd help me remember home. When my watch says 5 A.M., I know Dad is rollin' out to milk the cows. And any night when it says 7:30, I know the whole family's around

You don't raise heroes, you raise sons. And if you treat them like sons, they'll turn out to be heroes, even if it's just in your own eyes.

a well-spread table, and Dad's thankin' God for what's on it and askin' Him to watch over me. I can almost smell the hot biscuits and bacon.

"It's thinkin' about those things that makes me want to fight when the goin' gets tough," he concluded. "I can find out what time it is where I am easy enough. What I want to know is, what time it is in Utah."

This serviceman's father had obviously set good examples for his son and had raised him to appreciate home and family values. He had acquired such strong faith that he was willing to fight for his country to preserve it.[54]

As a father has compassion on his children, so the LORD has compassion on those who fear him.
PSALMS 103:13

> *The most important thing is not so much that every child should be taught, as that every child should be given the wish to learn.*

There was a man who played with his little boy after work each night. One day, he knew that he would have extra work that evening and wanted to be able to give his little boy something to do. Looking around his office, he saw a magazine with a large map of the world on the cover. He tore off the cover with the map and patiently ripped it up into small pieces to take to his son.

When he got home, his son came running to meet him. The man explained that he couldn't play just then, but had something else for him to do. He spread all the pieces out on the table and explained that it was a map of the world.

About thirty minutes later, the little boy came to his dad and said, "Okay, it's finished.

Can we play now?" Surprised, the man went to see the picture. Sure enough, there was the world, every piece in place.

The man said, "That's amazing! How did you do that?"

The little boy said, "It was simple. On the back of the page was a picture of a man. When I put the man together, the whole world fell into place."

One of the greatest gifts you can give to your children is the desire to learn about the world around them, about themselves, and about their Creator.[55]

Seek, and ye shall find; knock,
and it shall be opened unto you.
MATTHEW 7:7 KJV

Sometimes when nothing goes just right and worry reigns supreme,

When heartache fills the eyes with mist and all things useless seem,

There's just one thing can drive away the tears that scald and blind—

Someone to slip a strong arm 'round and whisper, "Never mind."

No one has ever told just why those words such comfort bring,

Nor why that whisper makes our cares depart on hurried wing.

> *Many who have spent a lifetime in love tell us less of it than the child who lost a dog yesterday.*

Yet troubles say a quick "Good-day," we leave them far behind

When someone slips an arm around, and whispers, "Never mind."

But love must prompt that soft caress—that love must, aye, be true

Or at that tender, clinging touch no heart ease come to you,

But if the arm be moved by love, sweet comfort you will find

When someone slips an arm around, and whispers, "Never mind!"

This poem reflects the comfort that only a loving touch can bring! Show your love for your children in the things you say and do. That love will be returned to you many times over.[56]

We should love one another.
1 JOHN 3:11

> *We discover our parents when we become parents ourselves.*

Janet spent the summer with her grandparents when she was ten. One day their neighbor, Audrey, came over to visit and introduce herself to Janet. She invited Janet to visit her anytime. Janet did, and they became fast friends. Audrey's children were grown, but her mothering nature wasn't ready to retire. Or perhaps God let her know how much Janet needed her nurturing, friendship, and wisdom.

As the two of them walked in the flower garden, Audrey explained each type of flower, somehow connecting it with wisdom about people. Then they would go into her house and have punch and cookies. They spent most of the summer

118

together talking, walking, shopping, and becoming dear friends.

Through the time Janet spent with Audrey, she learned how to love herself and others, and how to make life full and happy. She learned the value of friendship and loyalty, and that people need each other. "There's usually a good side to every bad situation—you just have to look for it," Audrey would tell Janet.

Janet is now a grandmother herself. To this day, she can still see Audrey's smiling face and hear her wise words laced with love.[57]

Grandchildren are the crown of the aged,
and the glory of children is their parents.
PROVERBS 17:6 NRSV

Journalist Bob Greene was often asked how it felt to be a new father. He recalls, "Normally, I shrug the question off; it's so complicated and so consuming that I don't feel I can do it justice with a glib reply. I usually just say, 'Yeah, its great!'"

One day he truly expressed to two friends how he felt and tells about it in his book *Good Morning, Merry Sunshine:*

A rose can say
I love you,
Orchids can enthrall,
But a weed bouquet
in a chubby fist,
Oh my, that says it all!

"I don't even know how to explain it. I've been spending time on the road ever since I started working for a living. I've complained about it a lot, but I've really liked the idea of it. Going into different cities, sleeping in hotels, meeting strange people . . . I've really liked it. Now, though, when I'm gone . . . I physically ache for missing my daughter. It never seems that any story is important enough to make me not see her for another day. I know I still go out on the road all the time—I wonder if I'm fooling myself—but missing her is not some vague concept in my mind. It actually hurts when I think that she's at home and I'm not with her. Sometimes I fall asleep thinking about it."

Parenthood arouses the deepest of emotions. Treasure your children today.[58]

The purposes of a man's heart are deep waters,
but a man of understanding draws them out.
PROVERBS 20:5

> *Life is the soul's nursery —*
> *its training place for the*
> *destinies of eternity.*

R. Lee Sharpe of Carrollton, Georgia, tells an interesting story that was published in the *Alabama Baptist:*

"I was just a kid," related Mr. Sharpe. "One spring day, Father called me to go with him to old man Trussell's blacksmith shop. He had left a rake and a hoe to be repaired. And there they were, ready, fixed like new. Father handed over a silver dollar for the repairing, but Mr. Trussell refused to take it. 'No,' he said, 'there's no charge for that little job.' But father insisted that he take the pay.

"If I live a thousand years," said Mr. Sharpe, "I'll never forget that great blacksmith's reply, 'Sid,' he said to my father, 'can't you let a man do something now and then just to stretch his soul?'

"It is the old law. The giver receives a reward. Bread cast upon the waters comes back. One who stretches his soul in deeds of love and kindness, unfailingly reaps a just reward."

Henry van Dyke once said, "We make a living by what we get, but we make a life by what we give." Our life here on earth is a training place for all eternity. Use the time wisely![59]

Hold on to instruction, do not let it go;
guard it well, for it is your life.
PROVERBS 4:13

Carolyn Hagan wrote an article in *Child* magazine that contained an interview with Pulitzer Prize-winning author Alice Walker. A portion of her story follows:

"When I was a little girl, I accidentally broke a fruit jar. Several brothers and a sister were nearby who could have done it. But my father turned to me and asked, 'Did you break the jar, Alice?'

The key to everything is patience. You get the chicken by hatching the egg, not by smashing it open.

"Looking into his large, brown eyes, I knew he wanted me to tell the truth. I also knew he might punish me if I did. But the truth inside of me wanted badly to be expressed. 'I broke the jar,' I said.

"The love in his eyes rewarded and embraced me. Suddenly I felt an inner peace that I still recall with gratitude to this day."

This was a parent who knew the value of patience in interacting with his children. He didn't yell and scream; he asked the question softly, hoping for the truth. Wonderful results occur when you discipline your children consistently and patiently. If you haven't tried this approach with your children, it might bring you unexpected joys in your relationship with them.[60]

For ye have need of patience.
HEBREWS 10:36 KJV

> *The great man is he who does not lose his child's heart.*

What are children? They are bundles of energy who stop running around and asking questions only when they are totally exhausted and drop off to sleep. They climb trees, dig around in streams, and generally run adults frazzled just watching them. Some are quieter than others, but they all ask questions. It does not matter to the child if this drives you to distraction or puts a big smile on your face. They "question" and "do" day in and day out.

Children behave this way because they want to know. They are like enormous dry sponges soaking in everything around them. It is a priceless moment when they see something special. Their faces light up like Christmas morning. Their eyes bulge open and mouths gape almost in disbelief, and then they smile. We adults have often forgotten how to smile.

Children don't hide a thing. If they are excited or scared, it is obvious. They accept and return love and care with reckless abandon. We may put away childish thinking, but there is a reward in experiencing the joy of a child.[61]

Unless you change and become like children, you will never enter the kingdom of heaven.
MATTHEW 18:3 NRSV

The best-selling products for Procter and Gamble in 1879 were candles. Because Thomas Edison had invented the light bulb, it looked as if candles might become obsolete and the company would be in trouble. Their fears became reality when the market for candles plummeted. The economic forecast for the company seemed bleak.

> *That energy which makes a child hard to manage is the energy that afterwards makes him a manager of life.*

However, about this time, a forgetful employee at a small factory in Cincinnati forgot to turn off his machine when he went to lunch. The result was a frothing mass of lather filled with air bubbles. He almost threw the mess away, but instead made it into soap. The soap floated, and thus Ivory soap was born. It became the mainstay of

Procter and Gamble. Destiny had played a dramatic part in pulling the struggling company out of bankruptcy.

Why was floating soap so special? During that time, some people bathed in the river. Floating soap would never sink, and as a result would not be lost. Ivory soap ultimately became a best-seller across the country.

Teach your children to use their energy and creativity to turn their mistakes into successes![62]

*Therefore encourage one another
and build each other up.*
1 THESSALONIANS 5:11

129

> *When you're dealing with a child, keep your wits about you, and sit on the floor.*

The following amusing story written by Billy Graham is called "Let Go."

"A little child was playing one day with a very valuable vase. He put his hand into it and could not withdraw it. His father, too, tried his best, but all in vain. They were thinking of breaking the vase when his father said, 'Now, my son, make one more try. Open your hand and hold your fingers out straight as you see me doing, and then pull.'

"To his astonishment the little fellow said, 'Oh no, Father. I couldn't put my fingers out like that, because if I did I would drop my penny.'"

This story has significant meaning for all of us who work with children. A child looks

130

at his surroundings with a different per-
spective from that of adults. The prospect of
losing the penny is more important to him
than the loss of the expensive vase. He
knows the penny's value to him in his
everyday life.

Children will continue to surprise all of
us by their reasoning processes, but if we're
patient and remember to "sit on the floor,"
we'll better understand them.[63]

Make the most of every opportunity.
COLOSSIANS 4:5

A father arrived home to find his daughters petitioning their mother for permission to go to a Friday-night birthday party that would run until midnight. However, they were due to attend an all-day music conference beginning early Saturday morning.

Children have to be educated, but they have also to be left to educate themselves.

"Can we go?" they pleaded. "We'll be fine on Saturday."

He was tired, so he brushed them off with a, "We'll talk in the morning."

"Okay," he announced the next morning, "you can go to the party tonight. But you might want to think about how hard you've worked the past three months getting ready for this competition. Do you want to jeopardize it? How late would you choose to stay?"

"How late can we stay?" Rhonda asked, putting the responsibility back on him.

"You tell me," he replied. "If you were on your own and I were out of the picture, when would you leave the party in order not to be dog-tired for Saturday?"

They looked at each other. All at once this wasn't a case of what Dad would allow, but rather what was in their best interest. Then came the most amazing answer of all: "We don't think we want to go to the party."[64]

My son, do not forget my teaching,
but keep my commands in your heart.
PROVERBS 3:1

The tongue is the deadliest of all blunt instruments.

Many analogies have been given for the "untamed tongue." Francis Quarles likened it to a drawn sword that takes a person prisoner: "A word unspoken is like the sword in the scabbard, thine; if vented, thy sword is in another's hand."

Others have described evil-speaking as:

- A freezing wind—one that seals up the sparkling waters and kills the tender flowers and shoots of growth. In similar fashion, bitter and hate-filled words bind up the hearts of men and cause love to cease to flourish.

- A fox with a firebrand tied to its tail sent out among the standing corn just as in the days of Samson and the Philistines. So gossip spreads without control or reason.

- A pistol fired in the mountains, the echo of which is intensified until it sounds like thunder.

Perhaps the greatest analogy is one given by a little child who came running to her mother in tears. "Did your friend hurt you?" the mother asked.

"Yes," said the girl.

"Where?" asked her mother.

"Right here," said the child, pointing to her heart.

Words have the power to hurt and tear down or heal and uplift. Ask God to help you place a guard on your tongue.[65]

Fathers, do not provoke your children,
or they may lose heart.
COLOSSIANS 3:21 NRSV

When Rosa Parks was arrested for sitting in the front of a bus in an area reserved for white passengers, the black people of Montgomery, Alabama, were angry. It was 1955, and segregation regarding public transportation, restrooms, drinking fountains, and other areas was rampant throughout the South.

> *The roots grow deep when the winds are strong.*

The 27-year-old minister of the Dexter Avenue Baptist Church in Montgomery met with other ministers to decide on a course of action. They urged their fellow blacks not to ride the city's buses on December 5th. However, the bus boycott lasted 382 days. The ministers repeatedly asked their congregations to remain peaceful and calm.

The young minister Martin Luther King Jr., was made famous internationally by the publicity surrounding the bus boycott. He became not only a spokesman for his community, but a target as well. A bomb exploded on his front porch. Although no one was injured, a crowd of more than a thousand people gathered in anger. King spoke from the smoking ruins of his porch, saying, "Be peaceful. I want you to love your enemies."

Martin Luther King Jr. was a man of deep convictions who did not waver in the face of hostility. First and foremost, he was a man of God. In like manner, teach your children to sink their roots deeply into the soil of God's Word. It will strengthen them for the challenges of life.[66]

If thou faint in the day of adversity,
thy strength is small.
PROVERBS 24:10 KJV

> *The most important thing a father can do for his children is to love their mother.*

Author and editor Kevin Miller, shares a decision he made based on the love he has for his wife and family. A few years ago, he was invited to join the board of a Christian organization. He believed in the work and wanted to help. Being asked to serve was a dream come true.

As he talked to his wife about the invitation, she pointed out all the Saturday meetings and evening phone calls that would come with the position. The family already felt stretched out, and the two of them had little time to spend alone together. She didn't think he should accept the invitation.

Mr. Miller did not want to hear her answer. For three days, he seesawed back and forth, unsure of what to do. What helped him make his decision was his prayer, "God, what specific things have You called me to do?"

One answer was, "Love your wife and children. Support them and help develop their gifts." If he joined the board, he realized he couldn't fulfill that successfully. He turned down the opportunity.

A husband's love for his wife and children and the importance of the family should be the deciding factor in any decision that would take an inordinate amount of time away from them.[67]

Where your treasure is,
there your heart will be also.
MATTHEW 6:21 NRSV

There is a legend surrounding Jonathan Edwards, one of America's greatest preachers as well as the third president of Princeton University, and his daughter. His daughter had an uncontrollable temper, although this fault was not known to many people outside of the family. Legend says that a young man fell in love with the preacher's daughter and asked to marry her.

> *People who fly into a rage always make a bad landing.*

"You can't have her," was Jonathan Edwards' abrupt answer.

"But I love her," replied the young man.

"You can't have her," repeated Edwards.

"But she loves me," the young man replied.

Again Edwards said, "You can't have her."

"Why?" asked the young man.

"Because she is not worthy of you."

"But," he asked, "she is a Christian, isn't she?"

"Yes, she is a Christian. But the grace of God can live with some people with whom no one else could ever live!"

Teach your children that temper tantrums are not acceptable behavior. Anger not only makes everyone else miserable, but it can affect the rest of their lives.[68]

It is better to be slow-tempered than famous; it is better to have self-control than to control an army.
PROVERBS 16:32 TLB

Listening to your children is like shopping in the bargain basement. You get a lot of things you didn't know you needed— and at a very good price.

One afternoon while playing on a wooden picnic table, a little boy ran a splinter into his finger. Sobbing, he called his father, who was a pastor, at his office. He said, "Daddy, I want God to take the splinter out."

The father said, "Go to your mother. She'll be able to remove it for you."

"No," the little boy insisted, "I want God to take it out."

"Why don't you trust your mother to do it?" his father asked.

"Because when Mommy takes a splinter out, it hurts. If God takes it out, it won't hurt."

When the father arrived home at the end of his workday, he found his son still nursing a sore and inflamed finger. In spite of his son's initial protests, the father proceeded to remove the splinter. The procedure was a bit painful, but the relief was complete.

Somehow, this little boy had gotten the impression that God's healing was painless and would not hurt him. Unfortunately, the healing process can be painful. This incident also teaches that God involves others in the healing process: parents, doctors, ministers, and counselors, just to name a few.[69]

He who has an ear, let him hear.
REVELATION 13:9

"Adversity is often the window of opportunity for change," Leith Anderson has said. "Few people or organizations want to change when there is prosperity and peace. Major changes are often precipitated by necessity."

> *There is no education like adversity.*

Petronius had a different outlook on the results of change. He said, "We trained hard . . . but every time we were beginning to form into teams we would be reorganized. I was to learn later in life that we tend to meet any new situation by reorganizing. What a wonderful method it can be for creating the illusion of progress while producing inefficiency and demoralization."

And Martin Luther King Jr. had a more spiritual opinion of adversity. "The ultimate measure of a man," he said, "is not where he stands in moments of comfort and convenience, but where he stands at times of challenge and controversy."

God loves us in good times and bad; what really matters is what happens in us and not to us. Sometimes God calms the storm—sometimes He lets the storm rage and calms His child.[70]

A just man falleth seven times,
and riseth up again.
PROVERBS 24:16 KJV

Children spell love t-i-m-e.

"There are little eyes upon you, and they are watching night and day;

There are little ears that quickly take in every word you say;

There are little hands all eager to do everything you do.

And a little boy who's dreaming of the day he'll be like you.

You're the little fellow's idol, you're the wisest of the wise,

In his little mind about you, no suspicions ever rise;

He believes in you devoutly, holds that all you say and do,

He will say and do in your way when he's grown up to be like you.

There's a wide-eyed little fellow who believes you're always right,

And his ears are always open and he watches day and night;

You are setting an example every day in all you do,

For the little boy who's waiting to grow up to be like you.

—Unknown

Children believe in their parents and want to be just like them. You're the most important people in their lives. They will remember the example you set for them as long as they live. Savor the time spent with your children and grandchildren. That is one of the greatest gifts you can give them.[71]

May the LORD bless you . . . all the days of your life . . . and may you live to see your children's children.
PSALMS 128:5-6

The king of retail was the late John Wanamaker. While walking through his store in Philadelphia one day, he noticed a customer waiting for assistance. There was no one paying the least bit of attention to her. Looking around, he saw his salespeople clustered together

> *The art of being wise is the art of knowing what to overlook.*

laughing and talking among themselves. Without a word, he softly slipped behind the counter and waited on the customer himself. Then he quietly handed the purchase to the salespeople to be wrapped as he went on his way.

Later, Wanamaker was quoted as saying, "I learned thirty years ago that it is foolish to scold. I have enough trouble overcoming my own limitations without fretting over the fact that God has not seen fit to distribute evenly the gift of intelligence."

If you nag at children, they often become resentful or learn to tune you out. Sometimes you can make a bigger impact by leaving some words unsaid.[72]

In the multitude of words there wanteth not sin: but he that refraineth his lips is wise.
PROVERBS 10:19 KJV

> *Self-control is the ability to stay cool when someone else is making you hot.*

A father was trying to teach his son, who had a bad temper, how to control it. He told his son, "Each time you lose your temper and blow up, I'm going to put a nail in the gate. When you accomplish something good, I'm going to take a nail out."

After a while, the boy saw that he was getting a lot of nails in the gate. He finally resolved that he was going to stop getting mad and learn to control his temper. Soon he noticed that the nails were getting fewer and fewer. Every time he did something good, his father took out more nails.

Finally, the boy had all the nails removed from the gate. His father came to him and said, "Son, I'm proud of you, but I want you

150

GOD'S LITTLE DEVOTIONAL BOOK FOR PARENTS

to remember something. All the nails are gone from this gate and that is very good. But the scars from those nails are still in the wood. God will forgive you for your bad temper, but you reap what you sow. When you see those scars, you will be reminded of the lesson you have learned."

Discipline is teaching your child to exercise self-control.[73]

Don't fail to correct your children;
discipline won't hurt them!
PROVERBS 23:13 TLB

Billy Graham tells of a time when he was in the hospital in Hawaii. While there, he read again of the appalling events that led up to the destruction of the United States naval fleet at Pearl Harbor. The Japanese air force attacked on Sunday, December 7, 1941, and the military bases on Oahu were left burning and in shambles. The

> *The young have no depth perception in time. Ten years back or ten years forward is an eternity.*

military had no warning of the impending catastrophe. It is now known that the attack was invited by our failure to be always vigilant. The shocking result was the destruction of our fleet—the cause was tragic indifference. Comfort, ease, and pleasure were put ahead of duty and conviction. When this happens, progress is always set back.

What makes us shrug our shoulders when we ought to be flexing our muscles? What makes us unresponsive in a day when there are loads to lift, a world to be won, and captives to be set free? Why are so many bored when the times demand action? Christ told us that in the last days there would be an insipid attitude toward life.

Give your children a vision for the future by helping them to understand our past![74]

Where there is no vision, the people perish.
PROVERBS 29:18 KJV

> *God will not demand more from you as a parent than what He will help you do.*

There is an old legend that says God first created birds without wings. In due time, God made wings and said to the birds, "Come, take up these burdens and bear them."

The birds hesitated at first, but soon obeyed. They tried picking up the wings in their beaks, but they were too heavy. Next they tried picking them up with their claws, but they were too large. At last one of the birds managed to lift the wings onto its shoulders where it was possible to carry them.

Before long, the wings began to grow and soon had attached themselves to the birds' bodies. One of the birds began to flap his wings and soar in the air above! Soon others followed his example. What had been a heavy burden now became the instrument that enabled the birds to go where they could never go before, truly fulfilling the destiny of their creation.

The duties and responsibilities that are entrusted to you as a parent are precious and many. Sometimes it feels like you will never get through the next day, much less the next year. The sleepless nights of late feedings and colic, the endless days of the "terrible twos," homework, parent conferences, preadolescence, and teenagers—all these combined can seem like a huge burden. However, remember the legend of the birds and their wings and know that God will be there for you.[75]

For with God nothing shall be impossible.
LUKE 1:37 KJV

There were once two warring tribes in the Andes, one living in the lowlands and the other high in the mountains. One day the mountain people invaded the lowlanders, kidnapping a baby. They took the infant with them back up into the mountains.

The lowlanders didn't know how to climb the mountain or how to track the mountain people in the steep terrain. Even so, they sent out their best party of fighting men to climb the mountain and bring the baby home. After several days of striving, however, they had climbed only several hundred feet.

> *Making the decision to have a child is momentous—it is to decide forever to have your heart go walking around outside your body.*

Feeling hopeless and helpless, the lowlander men decided that the cause was lost. As they prepared to return to their village below, they saw the baby's mother walking toward them. They realized that she was coming down the mountain that they hadn't figured out how to climb. And then they saw that she had the baby strapped to her back. How could that be?

One man greeted her and said, "We couldn't climb this mountain. How did you do this when we, the strongest and most able men in the village, couldn't do it?"

She shrugged her shoulders and said, "It wasn't your baby."[76]

And now faith, hope, and love abide, these three; and the greatest of these is love.
1 CORINTHIANS 13:13 NRSV

If it was going to be easy to raise kids, it never would have started with something called labor.

The Clark family, who lived in Scotland many years ago, had a dream. Mr. and Mrs. Clark worked and saved while making plans for themselves and their nine children to travel to the United States. It took years for them to save enough money, but they finally did it. They received passports and made reservations for the entire family to sail on a new ocean liner.

The whole family was filled with excitement and anticipation. However, a few days prior to their departure, a dog bit the youngest son. Due to the possibility of rabies, the Clarks were quarantined for fourteen days.

The family's dreams of going to America were destroyed. The father was filled with

158

disappointment and anger, blaming his son and God for their misfortune. He went to the dock without his family to watch the ship leave and shed his tears of regret.

Five days later, the tragic news spread throughout Scotland that the ship, the mighty Titanic, had sunk to the bottom of the sea. Mr. Clark hugged his son and thanked him and God for saving their lives. What he saw as a tragedy for his family had been turned into a blessing.[77]

He gives us more grace.
JAMES 4:6

During war games, Private Glenn Sollie and Private Andrew Bearshield of the Fifteenth Infantry were ordered to make their way to a bridge and stand guard until they were relieved.

The two were faithful soldiers. They went to the bridge and guarded it . . . and guarded it. They stuck to their job for three days and nights with neither food nor blankets. They eventually were found rather than "relieved." The two privates had been guarding the wrong bridge! They had lost their way and taken their battle stations at a bridge seven miles away from the one they were to guard. One might suppose they were reprimanded for making such a mistake. On the contrary, they were given military honors for guarding their position with such faithfulness!

If at first you don't succeed, relax; you're just like the rest of us.

All parents make mistakes with their children. Parenting is a profession in which you learn by doing. Focus on what you've done right, instead of blaming yourself for every wrong decision. God will honor you for your faithfulness![78]

Love never fails.
1 CORINTHIANS 13:8

> *Life isn't a matter of milestones, but of moments.*

A young mother was cleaning house one day. Coming downstairs with arms loaded with soiled sheets and towels, she nudged her way around two little bodies playing on the steps. *Why do children love stairs so much?* she thought, and asked them to excuse her.

They shifted positions a little, and she balanced her load on its way to the washer in the basement. She had not gone far when she heard a little voice pipe, "I love to come to your house. Your mother doesn't yell all the time the way my mother does."

The mother paused and suddenly realized that this little girl had been over to play frequently. She didn't know the little girl's mother, and didn't have any way to know what type of person she was. However, she did sense that this little girl had found a quiet place of shelter in her home.

Moments like this are building blocks for teaching your children. This young mother was creating for her children and their friends an example of patience and hospitality. An atmosphere of love, understanding, and acceptance creates a place in which children can feel safe and secure.[79]

*But encourage one another daily,
as long as it is called Today.*
HEBREWS 3:13

Once upon a time there was a young man who left home, denouncing his father and mother. He wanted nothing to do with them again. Yet years later, he felt led to return home to see his parents. He wrote a letter to his mother, begging for her forgiveness. He asked that if she would

> *We can do no great things—only small things with great love.*

let him come back home to hang a white handkerchief on the clothesline in the backyard. The train passed near the rear of their house, and he said that if the handkerchief were there as he passed by he would know that she would let him come home.

As he passed by on the train to his amazement, there was not a white handkerchief on the line, however a number of white sheets flapped in the breeze. How great was the love of that mother for her son! It was a small thing to hang sheets on the line, but what great love it conveyed!

A mother's heart is always big enough to hold the love she has for all her children and the forgiveness for the wrongs done and said by them. That capacity for forgiveness is a part of a mother's love, just as it is in God's love for us.[80]

Let all that you do be done in love.
1 CORINTHIANS 16:14 NRSV

> *It's the three pairs of eyes that mothers have to have . . . one pair that sees through closed doors . . . another in the back of her head . . . and, of course, the ones in front that can look at a child when he goofs up and reflect, "I understand and I love you" without so much as uttering a word.*

No matter how much some of us try, we just cannot do without Mother. Father loves her, daughter imitates her, and son ignores her. She likes sewing, detective stories, having her birthday remembered, church, a new dress, the cleaning woman, Father's praise, flowers and plants, dinner out on Sunday, crossword puzzles, sunny days, tea, and the newspaper boy.

She dislikes having her birthday forgotten, spring-cleaning, Junior's report card, rainy days, and the neighbor's dog.

She can be found standing by, bending over, reaching for, kneeling under, and stretching around, but rarely sitting on.

She has the beauty of a spring day, the patience of a saint, and the memory of an elephant.

She knows everybody's birthday, what you should be doing, and all your secret thoughts.

She is always straightening up after, reminding you to, and taking care of, but never asking for.

Yes, a mother is one person whom nobody can do without. And when you have harassed her, buffeted her about, tried her patience, and worn her out, you can win her back with four little words: Mom, I love you![81]

Her children arise and call her blessed;
her husband also, and he praises her.
PROVERBS 31:28

Mothers have been teaching their children since time began. Many famous individuals have attributed their accomplishments to the teachings of their mothers.

George Washington's mother taught him the biblical ideals of political and social morality which Washington kept before

> *The mother's heart is the child's schoolroom.*

the nation throughout his life. The family held prayers twice a day with regular readings from the Scriptures.

Ferdinand Foch was a great general of World War II. It was said of him, "General Foch is a man of prayer, a prophet whom God inspires." His mother taught him to put his faith in God and pray. He continued the habits he learned while living in his mother's home.

The mother of Dwight Moody was a widow who struggled against poverty on a New

England farm, but she took the time to teach her son the importance of eternal values.

Oliver Cromwell's mother taught him the simple truths of Scripture. He chose as his favorite verse, "I can do all things through Christ which strengtheneth me." And William Penn, taught by his mother the importance of faith, took as his life text, "This is the victory, even our faith which overcometh the world."

A mother's words can have eternal value.[82]

She speaks with wisdom, and faithful instruction is on her tongue.
PROVERBS 31:26

> *Becoming a father is easy enough, but being one can be rough.*

A pastor shared a personal story in *New Man* magazine regarding his disobedient daughter. She had given birth out of wedlock and was now chafing at the house rules set by her parents. She was warned that breaking their evening curfew had strict consequences.

In the middle of the night, the pastor awoke to the sound of the doorbell ringing. He rushed downstairs. It was his daughter standing on the porch, begging him, "Daddy, Daddy, let me in."

He saw his grandson next to his daughter. He pointed to his watch and closed the curtain. She continued to bang and ring, waking everyone in the house.

"Daddy, let her in," his youngest daughter pleaded.

"Haman, the baby is out there," his wife pleaded.

"No," he said. "If we hold the line now, we won't have to do this again."

He wondered about the risk he was taking. His wife and younger daughter begged him to reconsider, but he firmly stood. Finally, his daughter gave up and spent the night at a friend's house. By the next morning, she had decided to submit to the house rules. Her family warmly welcomed her back.

It's sometimes necessary to demonstrate "tough love," even when it feels as though your heart is breaking.[83]

The LORD disciplines those he loves.
HEBREWS 12:6

A little boy and his big sister went out for a walk one day, and they decided to take a shortcut home by walking through a long, narrow railroad tunnel. For safety reasons, the railroad company had built small clefts next to the track in the tunnel so that if people got caught when a train was passing through they might save themselves.

The cure for fear is faith.

The little boy and girl had walked some distance into the tunnel when they heard a train coming. They were frightened at first, but the sister put her little brother in one cleft and she hurried and hid in another. As the train came thundering toward them, the sister cried out, "Johnny, cling close to the rock!"

After the train had passed through the tunnel, the sister went to retrieve her brother. They both were safe.

When the train of life is barreling toward you in a dark tunnel—when your problems seem overwhelming—cling to the Rock. His name is Jesus Christ. The Bible says that God is our refuge and our strength. Won't you trust in Him today?[84]

For God hath not given us the spirit of fear; but of power, and of love, and of a sound mind.
2 TIMOTHY 1:7 KJV

> *One today is worth
> two tomorrows.*

After having spent several months in a therapy group, Stuart decided to visit his twenty-year-old son at college. He asked Kevin what it had been like to have him as a father.

"Well, Dad," he said, "I don't want to hurt your feelings . . . but you were never there."

"What do you mean?" Stuart asked. "I was there every evening. I never went anywhere!"

Kevin said, "I know, Dad, but it was like there was nothing to you. You never got mad. If you were ever sad, I never knew it. You never seemed happy. I didn't know who you were. You were like a stranger to me most of the time. I felt like I didn't have a father."

When Stuart went back to his therapy sessions, he told the group what his son had said. He cried for the first time in more than forty years. "Can you believe it?" he asked. "I was there, and he felt I was invisible."

In time Stuart worked past this incident and experienced real emotional growth. He took his son deep-sea fishing and white-water rafting, experiencing the enjoyment of the moment with Kevin. His main regret was that he had wasted so much time in the past, hurting his son in the process, because there was so little inside of him for his son to know. It is never too late. Spend time with your children and show them the real you.[85]

By wisdom a house is built, and through understanding it is established.
PROVERBS 24:3-4

A young girl and her sisters went to live with their grandparents after their parents divorced. Their grandma taught them how to read, cook, and sew. She taught them when to plant and when to weed; how to forgive, laugh, and cry. They looked up to her as their role model.

The best things you can give children, next to good habits, are good memories.

After the sisters grew up and moved away, their grandma looked forward to their calls and visits. They valued them, too, because the older they got, the more they discovered they needed her advice. Grandma was their living home-and-garden encyclopedia, lovingly sharing her knowledge. They giggled when one sister telephoned for consolation over her lumpy homemade noodles, or when another needed to know how deep to plant tulip bulbs.

There was a big hole left in all their lives when Grandma died. They realized at the funeral that none of them ever left empty-handed or downhearted after a visit back home. Each always took away a recipe, a book, a doily pattern, a laugh, or just the awareness of how much she loved them.

This grandmother gave her granddaughters love, security, and good memories to sustain them after she was gone. How can we do any less for our families?[86]

I remember the days of long ago;
I meditate on all your works and
consider what your hands have done.
PSALMS 143:5

> *Remember, when they have a tantrum, don't have one of your own.*

A little boy moved with his parents to a house overlooking a deep canyon. One day his mother scolded him for disobeying her, and he became very angry. He stormed out of the house and ran to the edge of the canyon. He shouted as loud as he could, "I hate you! I hate you!"

Almost instantly, an angry, hollow shout came rushing back at him. "I hate you! I hate you!"

Surprised at first and then frightened, the little boy went running back to the house. Once safe in his mother's arms, he told her there was a bad man in the canyon who hated him and wanted to hurt him.

The wise mother took her son by the hand and led him back to the edge of the canyon. In a kind and cheerful voice, she called, "I love you! I love you!"

A tender, happy voice echoed back the same sweet words, much to the little boy's comfort and delight.

A child's tantrums can easily upset and anger us. Change the mood of the moment by responding in a positive, loving manner.[87]

Those with good sense are slow to anger,
and it is their glory to overlook an offense.
PROVERBS 19:11 NRSV

Tom attended the best schools in Augusta, but he always considered his real instructor to be his father. Long before the age when most boys are studying, young Tom was receiving from his father an education that was highly varied, extremely practical, and exceptionally sound academically.

Father and son were constant companions, but Sunday afternoons were chiefly

> *One father is worth more than a hundred schoolmasters.*

devoted to young Tom's training. While Tom sat on the floor or reclined against an inverted chair, his father poured into Tom's spellbound ears the tales of his own experience, learning, and thought. Tom's father was a man of in-depth information on the affairs of the world, literature, and theology. He coupled a robust imagination with an ability to reason clearly and focus on facts.

Tom eventually earned a doctorate of his own and became president of Princeton University. He was also elected governor of New Jersey. By the time he was elected President of the United States and became the foremost architect of the League of Nations, he had dropped entirely the use of his first name, Thomas. We know him in history simply as Woodrow Wilson.

Share your world with your children. Let them use that knowledge as a basis for future growth.[88]

Those who are wise will shine
like the brightness of the heavens.
DANIEL 12:3

> *Children are unpredictable.*
> *You never know what inconsistency*
> *they're going to catch you in next.*

A man tells of an incident that happened to him as a teenager. As he entered the seventh grade, his family moved to a new place. He decided to try out for the school chorus during the first week of classes. Since he already participated in the church choir, singing sounded like a great way to make friends and have fun. As he gently opened the door to the music room, the singing and laughter stopped as everyone stared at him—the new kid.

The teacher summoned him to the piano and handed him a piece of music. She started playing, with the expectation that he would sing. Reading unfamiliar music while trying to sing was nearly impossible, and it was obvious by the looks and snickers of the other children that he was not doing well. The next words out of the teacher's mouth devastated what little self-esteem he still possessed. "I'm sorry. You are not qualified to sing in our school chorus."

Words can hurt! But they can also heal. Twenty years later, a choir director walked up to this same man and said, "I heard you singing during worship today and really liked the sound of your voice. Would you be interested in joining our choir?"[89]

Reckless words pierce like a sword,
but the tongue of the wise brings healing.
PROVERBS 12:18

In the spring of 1871, a young man by the name of Sir William Osler picked up a book and read twenty-one words that had a profound effect on his future. A medical student at the Montreal General Hospital, he was worried about passing the final examination and about what to do, where to go, how to build up a practice, and how to make a living.

> *Never show a child what he cannot see. While you are thinking about what will be useful to him when he is older, talk to him of what he can use now.*

The twenty-one words that this young medical student read helped him become the most famous physician of his generation. He organized the world-famous John Hopkins School of Medicine. Here are the words from Thomas Carlyle that helped him lead a life free from worry: "Our main business is not to see what lies dimly at a distance, but to do what lies clearly at hand."

Children do not understand time as adults do. A child of five usually knows yesterday, today, and tomorrow. As they mature, they come to understand the idea of time more completely. This process can't be hurried, just as the process of learning to walk can't be rushed. It is an element of human development. Teach your children the things they need to know now; the rest will follow.[90]

A fool uttereth all his mind: but
a wise man keepeth it in till afterwards.
PROVERBS 29:11 KJV

185

Discipline is a proof of our sonship.

A grandfather once found his grandson, Joey, jumping up and down in his playpen, crying at the top of his voice. When Joey saw his grandfather, he stretched out his chubby hands and cried all the louder, "Out, Gamba, out!"

Naturally, the grandfather reached down to lift Joey out, but as he did, Joey's mother said, "No, Joey, you are being punished, so you must stay in your playpen."

The grandfather felt at a loss as to what to do. On the one hand, he knew he must comply with the mother's efforts to discipline her son. On the other hand, Joey's tears and uplifted hands tugged at his heart. Love found a way! If Gamba couldn't take his grandson out of the playpen, he could climb in and join him there!

Discipline in its finest form is "directing a child toward a better way." Discipline goes beyond punishment by instilling the desire never to repeat the misdeed, and instead make a better choice. The desire to do right is born of love—the love of the child for the parent, and more importantly, the love of the parent shown to the child.

Love your children enough to instill within them values to last a lifetime.[91]

Whoever loves discipline loves knowledge,
but he who hates correction is stupid.
PROVERBS 12:1

In a Los Angeles park, Roy B. Zuck saw a large tree that had grown somewhat crooked. The oddest thing about the tree was that someone had placed an upright pole near it and tied it to the tree with ropes. But the tree had grown out so far from the place where the trunk came out of the ground that there was a lot of distance between the pole and the tree. It was too late for this fix to help the tree.

> *Parents who are afraid to put their foot down usually have children who step on their toes.*

This often happens in the raising of children when parents allow them to run wild for the first fifteen years of their lives. When the parents realize their mistakes and try to correct or straighten out their children, sometimes they find that it's too late without intervention from an outside source.

Children require regular and consistent discipline. It creates limits and shows children that someone cares enough about them to set them on the right path. It is also a part of a loving relationship with your children and is necessary in helping them become responsible adults.[92]

He who heeds discipline shows the way to life, but whoever ignores correction leads others astray.
PROVERBS 10:17

> *You are the bow from which your children, as living arrows, are sent forth.*

When Harvey was a kid in Minnesota, watermelon was a delicacy. One of his father's friends, Bernie, was a prosperous fruit-and-vegetable wholesaler, who operated a warehouse in St. Paul.

Every summer, Bernie would call when the first watermelons came in. Harvey and his dad would go to Bernie's warehouse and take up their positions. They would sit on the edge of the dock, feet dangling, and lean over to lessen the volume of juice they were about to spill on themselves. Bernie would crack their first watermelon with his machete, hand them both a big piece, and sit down next to them. They would eat only the heart of the melon and throw away the rest.

Bernie was Harvey's father's idea of a rich man, and Harvey always thought it was because he was such a successful businessman. Years later he realized that what his father really admired about Bernie was his ability to stop working, get together with friends, and eat only the heart of the watermelon. He learned from Bernie that being rich is a state of mind. Some people will never have enough money to eat only the heart of the melon; others are rich without ever being more than one paycheck ahead.

Take time today to dangle your feet over the dock and chomp into life's small pleasures![93]

I have no greater joy than this, to hear that my children are walking in the truth.
3 JOHN 1:4 NRSV

A mother remembers one summer day when her nine-year-old son and a friend were getting a bottle of juice from the refrigerator. She had spent hours that morning scrubbing, waxing, and polishing the kitchen floor, so she cautioned the boys not to spill anything. They tried so hard to be careful that they accidentally bumped a tray of eggs on the door shelf, splattering eggs all over her clean floor.

> *A torn jacket is soon mended, but hard words bruise the heart of a child.*

The boys eyes widened with alarm as she exploded angrily. "Get out of here—now!" she shouted as they headed for the door.

By the time she had finished cleaning up the mess, she had calmed down. To make amends, she set a tray of cookies on the table along with the juice and some glasses.

But when she called the boys, there was no answer. They had gone somewhere else to play, someplace where her angry voice couldn't reach them.

Sometimes we forget how devastating our angry words can be to a child. Anger separates us from those we love. It shatters that intimate relationship that all of us desire to share with our families. Ask for God's help in keeping your anger under control.[94]

An angry man stirs up dissension, and
a hot-tempered one commits many sins.
PROVERBS 29:22

> *It is almost always through fear of being criticized that people tell lies.*

A twelve-year-old boy was the key witness in an important lawsuit. The attorney had put the boy through a rigorous cross-examination and had been unable to shake his concise, damaging testimony. He had given clear answers to all questions that he was asked.

In a stern voice, the attorney asked, "Your father has been telling you how to testify, hasn't he?"

"Yes," said the boy.

"Now," said the attorney with smug satisfaction, "just tell us what your father told you to say."

"Well," replied the boy, "Father told me that the lawyers may try to tangle me, but if

GOD'S LITTLE DEVOTIONAL BOOK FOR PARENTS

I would just be careful and tell the truth, I could say the same thing every time."

This boy's father had taught him an important lesson. Because he followed his father's advice, he was able to give clear testimony in the courtroom. When we follow our heavenly Father's lessons from the Bible, we will speak honestly with others in the same way as this young boy. What an example to follow! May we all have the courage to be honest even when our fear is great.[95]

An honest answer is like a kiss on the lips.
PROVERBS 24:26

If I had My Child to Raise All Over Again

If I had my child to raise all over again,

I'd build self-esteem first, and the house later.

I'd finger paint more, and point the finger less.

> *Children listen with their hearts.*

I would do less correcting and more connecting.

I'd take my eye off my watch, and watch with my eyes.

I would care to know less and know to care more,

I'd take more hikes and fly more kites.

I'd stop playing serious, and seriously play.

I would run through more fields and gaze at more stars.

I'd do more hugging and less tugging.

I'd see the oak tree in the acorn more often, and affirm much more.

I'd model less about the love of power,

And more about the power of love.

—Unknown

Live your life each day as though it were your last. The time spent with your children can't be regained next week, next month, or next year. Remember to spend it wisely.[96]

Teach them [God's commandments]
to your children, talking about them when
you are at home and when you are away,
when you lie down and when you rise . . .
So that your days and the days of
your children may be multiplied.
DEUTERONOMY 11:19,21 NRSV

> *He who gives to me
> teaches me to give.*

Arthur's father had to give an order only once, and one of his commandments was, "There's to be no hanging around. If he ain't workin' or someplace special, a man is supposed to be home."

Arthur and his brother were taught to work hard and love the family. Arthur's dad also said, "You gain by helping others." To match deed to word, he would take his sons with him to deliver food, wood, and old clothes to families in need. He also said, "You don't get nowhere by making enemies." Arthur never forgot.

As an internationally celebrated tennis player, Arthur Ashe arose at five o'clock on summer days, hit five hundred balls, ate

198

breakfast, and then hit five hundred more. He was known for his drive on the court and his gentleman's disposition off the court. He built a strong family. His wife, Jeanne, and his daughter, Camera, were the light of his life. He started the Safe Passage Foundation to help disadvantaged youth improve their scholastic skills and also teach them golf, tennis, and fencing. Throughout his adult life, he fought to bring blacks and whites closer together.

What Arthur Ashe Sr. said, he did. And so, too, Arthur Ashe Jr.[97]

Therefore be imitators of God as dear children. And walk in love, as Christ also has loved us and given Himself for us, an offering and a sacrifice to God for a sweet-smelling aroma.
EPHESIANS 5:1-2 NKJV

A father lost his temper one morning and unleashed his anger on his son who happened to be the closest target. Later in the day while he and his son were fishing, he felt guilty about what he had done. He began, "Son, I was a little impatient this morning."

> *Words can wound. Always count down before blasting off.*

"Uh huh," the son grunted, reeling in his line and preparing to cast again.

The father continued, "Uh . . . I realize I was a little hard to be around."

Again, "Uh huh" was the only response his son made.

The father continued, "I . . . I want you to know that, uh . . . I feel bad about it." Then, quick to excuse himself, he added, "But you know, son, there are times when I'm like that."

The boy merely said, "Uh huh."

A few seconds passed, and then the boy added, "You know, Dad. God uses you to teach all of us in the family patience."

Our families have a way of nailing us with their honesty. Accept the good advice they give.[98]

Be very careful, then, how you live—
not as unwise but as wise, making
the most of every opportunity.
EPHESIANS 5:15-16

> *The heart that loves
> is always young.*

Blessed is the child who has someone who understands that childhood's grief is real and calls for understanding and sympathy.

Blessed is the child who has someone who believes in him, to whom he can carry his problems unafraid.

Blessed is the child who has about him those who realize his need of Christ as Savior and will lead him patiently and prayerfully to the place of acceptance.

Blessed is the child who is allowed to pursue his curiosity into every worthwhile field of information.

Blessed is the child whose love of the true, the beautiful, and the good has been nourished throughout the years.

Blessed is the child whose innate imagination has been turned into channels of creative effort.

Blessed is the child who has learned freedom from selfishness through responsibility and cooperation with others.

Blessed is the child whose efforts to achieve have found encouragement and compassionate praise.

Blessed is the child who is loved.

A child who lives in the above atmosphere of acceptance, love, and accountability is indeed fortunate and should grow into a responsible adult capable of accomplishing great things.[99]

Love is patient, love is kind. . . .
It always protects, always trusts,
always hopes, always perseveres.
1 CORINTHIANS 13:4,7

Author Colleen Townsend Evans has written, "Silence need not be awkward or embarrassing, for to be with one you love, without the need for words, is a beautiful and satisfying form of communication.

"I remember times when our children used to come running to me, all of them chattering at once about the events of their day—and it was wonderful to have them share their feelings with me. But there were also the times when they came to me wanting only to be held, to have me stroke their heads and caress them into sleep. And so it is, sometimes, with us and with God our Father."

> *God's voice is heard in the silences.*

Don't make your children talk to you. Give them the respect and space to remain silent. Sometimes children need to work out their own opinions and ideas in quiet before voicing them. On the other hand, when they do talk, take time to listen carefully, intently, and kindly. By your doing this, your children will know that they can talk to you whenever they want.[100]

The LORD is compassionate and gracious,
slow to anger, abounding in love.
PSALMS 103:8

> ## There is no panic in trust.

John Croyle told the following story in *Focus on the Family* magazine:

One day, a father took his children for a boat ride. They were traveling downriver when suddenly, the motor stopped. When the father looked behind him, he noticed the red sweater tangled up in the propeller. Then his young son yelled, "Sherry fell in!"

In horror the father saw his little girl entwined in the propeller of the boat. She was submerged just beneath the surface of the water, looking straight into the eyes of her father and holding her breath. He jumped into the water and tried to push the motor up, but the heavy engine wouldn't budge. Time was running out. Desperately, the father filled his own lungs with air and dipped below the surface. Then he took a knife and quickly cut the sweater from the propeller and lifted his daughter into the boat. She was rushed to the hospital.

When the crisis was over, the doctors and nurses asked the girl, "How come you didn't panic?"

"Well, we've grown up on the river," Sherry said, "and my dad always taught us that if you panic, you die. Besides, I knew my daddy would come and get me."[101]

The Lord is my strength and my shield;
my heart trusts in him, and I am helped.
PSALMS 28:7

Years ago a professor gave a group of graduate students an assignment. Take two hundred boys between the ages of twelve and sixteen from the slums and investigate their background and environment. Then predict their chances for the future.

> *Education is not the filling of a pail, but the lighting of a fire.*

After compiling much data, the students concluded that 90 percent of the boys would spend some time in jail.

Twenty-five years later, another group of graduate students went back to the same area. They were able to get in touch with 180 of the original 200. They found that only four of the group had ever been sent to jail.

Why was it that these men, who had lived in a breeding place of crime, had such surprisingly good records? The researchers were continually told: "Well, there was a teacher. . . ."

They pressed further and found that in 75 percent of the cases, it was the same teacher. The researchers went to this woman who was now living in a home for retired teachers. Could she give them any reason why these boys should have remembered her?

"No," she said, "no, I really couldn't." And then, thinking back over the years, she said thoughtfully more to herself than to her questioners: "I loved those boys."

As parents, you are the first and best teachers your children could ever have.[102]

Train a child in the way he should go, and when he is old he will not turn from it.
PROVERBS 22:6

> *A youth is a person
> who is going to carry on
> what you have started.*

When Ocean Robbins and Ryan Eliason met at a summer camp in California, they were just teenagers. However, they shared a common dream of making a difference for the environment. They acted to bring their dream to reality by founding an organization called YES! (Youth for Environmental Sanity!). Robbins and Eliason created several comic skits, formed a rock band, and produced their own videos, which have been presented to more than a half-million teens in thirty-eight states. Their music presentations have inspired other teenagers to become involved with environmental issues.

Robbins and Eliason's friendship resulted in more than $100,000 being raised for environmental needs their first year. Since that time, YES! has sponsored several summer camps for teenagers who are interested in learning more about the environment. These two young men used their talents of organization, musical ability, and love of the environment to influence others to care about the earth's finite resources.

Help your children to consider their friendships carefully and choose those who will help them succeed in bringing hope and encouragement to others. Together, you can make a difference in the world around you.[103]

Teach these things. Don't let anyone
look down on you because you are young,
but set an example for the believers in speech,
in life, in love, in faith and in purity.
1 TIMOTHY 4:11-12

A woman attended her twenty-year high school reunion. It didn't seem possible that so many years had passed since she graduated. She was excited at the prospect of seeing those teachers and friends who had meant so much to her.

> *The people who influence you are people who believe in you.*

At the reunion, she encountered her freshman art teacher. She told him that she decided to go to college as a result of his inspiration and that she was now an art professor at a large state university. At the end of the evening's festivities, the high school art teacher searched out his former student. He shook her hand and said, "Thank you for saying those nice things about my teaching. You've really made my day."

"You're welcome," said the woman as she hugged him, "But let me thank you. You've made my life!"

Parents, teachers, and other adults have tremendous influence on a child's future. Children require nurturing over a long period of time in all the small day-to-day matters to gain the confidence to make wise decisions as they move into adulthood.[104]

*Instruct a wise man and he will
be wiser still, teach a righteous man
and he will add to his learning.*
PROVERBS 9:9

> *It is only in love that the unequal can be made equal.*

A Sunday school superintendent was registering two new boys into Sunday school. She asked their ages and birthdays so she could place them in the appropriate classes. The bolder of the two replied, "We're both seven. My birthday is April 8th and my brother's birthday is April 20th."

The superintendent replied, "But that's not possible, boys."

The quieter brother spoke up. "No, its true. One of us is adopted."

"Oh?" asked the superintendent, not convinced. "Which one?"

The two brothers looked at each other and smiled. The bolder one said, "We asked Dad that same question a while ago, but he

214

just looked at us and said he loved us both the same, and he couldn't remember anymore which one of us was adopted."

What a wonderful likeness of God's love! The Apostle Paul wrote: "Now if we are [God's] children, then we are heirs—heirs of God and co-heirs with Christ. . . ." (See Romans 8:17.) In essence, as adopted sons and daughters of God, we share completely in the inheritance of His Son, Jesus. If our heavenly Father can love us on an equal basis with His Son, surely we can love our children the same way and show no preference in the blessings or privileges we extend to them.[105]

But when the right time came, the time God decided on, he sent his Son, born of a woman, born as a Jew, to buy freedom for us who were slaves to the law so that he could adopt us as his very own sons.
GALATIANS 4:4-5 TLB

A young mountain climber, accompanied by two strong and experienced guides, was making his first climb in the Swiss Alps. The young man was well prepared for the climb physically, and he felt secure with one guide a-head of him and the other following.

For hours they climbed. Breathless and weary, they finally

> What you are is
> God's gift to you.
> What you make of
> yourself is your
> gift to Him.

reached the rocks protruding through the snow at the summit. The guide leading the way stepped aside for the last few yards of the ascent so that the young mountain climber might have his first glimpse of the view—a wonderful panorama of snow-capped peaks and the bright, cloudless sky.

Clambering up the rocks, the young man leaped to the top. The guide quickly grabbed hold of him and pulled him down. The young man had no way of knowing that fierce gales often blew across the summit rocks with winds strong enough to push him off balance. The guide quickly informed him of the dangers, saying, "On your knees, sir! You are never safe here except on your knees!"

This young man discovered that even though he thought he had prepared well for this climb, he still had more to learn. Life is full of mistakes; the danger is in not learning from them.[106]

Perseverance must finish its work
so that you may be mature and
complete, not lacking anything.
JAMES 1:4

> We are far more liable to
> catch the vices than the
> virtues of our associates.

There is a story of a man now grown old who had graduated from one of the Ivy League colleges. In his latter years, he had given much thought to those days of his youth—the delights, the hurts, the rights, and the wrongs that had been done. He became concerned about one of the college pranks they had played.

After a particularly exciting football game, he and a group of other young men had driven through some of the nearby towns and had changed all the signs at the commons. He wondered how many people had gone down the wrong roads because of them. How many accidents might have happened, and as a result, how many people had been injured? Those were statistics that he would probably never know.

Many young people go along with their friends' ideas of fun. They don't see any harm in their actions. However, every action has consequences. The same is true of our behavior as parents. Choose your associates carefully. Your children are always watching . . . and learning.[107]

Do not be misled: "Bad company corrupts good character."

1 CORINTHIANS 15:33

In the *New York Times,* Larry Dorman relates a story about the young golfer Tiger Woods and the source of his mental toughness.

His father, Earl Woods, traces it to an incident that occurred in 1992 when Tiger was sixteen. Tiger was playing in the Junior Orange Bowl

> *The most important thing that parents can teach their children is how to get along without them.*

Tournament in Miami. He was, as his father remembers it, "a little full of himself," and when things went badly for him, he started to pout. Then Tiger went into a slump and stopped trying. Mr. Woods, a former Green Beret, scolded his son.

"I asked him who he thought he was," Earl said. "I told him golf owed him nothing and that he had better not ever quit again."

The way his father recalls it, Tiger never said a word. And he never quit again.

Tiger's father knew that talent alone wouldn't get him where he wanted to go. It took Tiger patience, perseverance, and the remembrance of all the lessons learned on the journey to adulthood.

Most importantly, success involves parents teaching their children how to climb the steps of maturity and complete the journey on their own.[108]

Watch yourselves closely so that you do not forget the things your eyes have seen or let them slip from your heart . . . Teach them to your children and to their children after them.

DEUTERONOMY 4:9

> *Children repeat in the streets what they hear at the dinner table.*

During his tenure as president of Princeton University, Woodrow Wilson was once asked to speak to a group of parents. He said, "I get many letters from you parents about your children. You want to know why we people up here in Princeton can't make more out of them and do more for them. Let me tell you the reason we can't. It may shock you just a little, but I am not trying to be rude. The reason is that they are your sons, reared in your homes, blood of your blood, bone of your bone. They have absorbed the ideals of your homes. You have formed and fashioned them. They are your sons. In those malleable, moldable years of their lives, you have forever left your imprint upon them."

Many parents fail to realize that a child will rarely exhibit a higher standard of morality, godliness, and ambition than that displayed by the parents. We can never expect others to convey to our children that which only we as parents can give and do.

You are the main "star" in your child's life. All others are supporting actors.[109]

For the value of wisdom is far above rubies; nothing can be compared with it.
PROVERBS 8:11 TLB

A Teenager's Plea

When I ask you to listen to me and you start giving me advice, you have not done what I asked. When I ask you to listen to me and you begin to tell me why I shouldn't feel that way, you are trampling on my feelings. When I ask

> *In case of doubt, it is better to say too little than too much.*

you to listen to me and you feel you have to do something to resolve my problem, you have failed me, strange as that may seem.

Listen! All I asked was that you listen, not to talk or do—just hear me. I can do for myself. I am not helpless. When you do something for me that I can and need to do for myself, you contribute to my fear and inadequacy. But when you accept as a simple fact that I do feel what I feel no matter how irrational, then I can quit trying to convince you and can get to the business of understanding what's behind this irrational feeling.

And when that's clear, the answers are obvious.

Perhaps that's why prayer works—because God listens in silence.[110]

There is a time for everything.
A time to be silent, and a time to speak.
ECCLESIASTES 3:1,7

> *To instill a healthy prayer life in your children, pray yourself.*

"You must have a good heart," one man said to his child, "if you are going to act right in this world." He continued, "Suppose my watch was not keeping time very well. Would it do any good if I went to the town clock and made the hands of my watch point exactly the same as those of the larger clock in the square? No, of course not! Rather, I should take my watch to a watchmaker or jewelry store that repairs watches. It is only when my watch has been cleaned and repaired that its hands will be able to keep time accurately all day long."

When we spend time in prayer, we are going to the Heart Maker, asking Him to clean and repair our hearts from the damage caused by the wrong things we have done. We are asking Him to put us right again on the inside so that we can more clearly determine right from wrong.

When our children see us in prayer, they are much more likely to go to God when they feel their own lives are in turmoil, rather than turning to the world and resetting their souls according to its standards and priorities.[111]

Evening, and morning, and at noon, will I pray, and cry aloud: and he shall hear my voice.
PSALMS 55:17 KJV

Legend has it that a missionary was swept overboard while traveling on rough seas and was washed up on a beach at the edge of a remote native village. Nearly dead from expo- sure and lack of food and fresh water, he was found by the people of the village

> *Well done is better than well said.*

and nursed back to health. He lived among them for twenty years, quietly adapting to their culture and working alongside them. He preached no sermons and neither read nor recited scripture to them.

But when people were sick, he sat with them—sometimes all night. When people were hungry, he fed them. When people were lonely, he listened. He taught the uneducated and always took the side of the one who had been wronged.

The day came when missionaries entered this village and began talking to the people about a man named Jesus. After listening for a while to their story, the native people began insisting that Jesus had already been living in their village for many years. "Come," one of them said, "we'll introduce you to Him."

The missionaries were led to a hut where they found their long-lost friend!

We are known by what we do and the example we set for others. Let the light of Christ shine forth in your life.[112]

Show me your faith without deeds, and
I will show you my faith by what I do.
JAMES 2:18

> One example is worth
> a thousand arguments.

Cal Ripken Jr. broke a baseball record on September 6, 1995, that many believed would never be broken. It was for the number of consecutive games he had played in, and on that date he broke Lou Gehrig's record of 2,131 games. He gave much of the credit for his success to the example and teaching of his father, Cal Ripken Sr., who coached and managed for the Orioles.

Ripken Sr. was inducted into the Orioles Hall of Fame during the 1996 season. His son gave a testimonial speech during the awards ceremony. To describe his relationship with his father, Cal Jr. told a little story about his two children, Rachel, age six, and Ryan, age three.

"They'd been bickering for weeks, and one day I heard Rachel taunt Ryan, 'You're just trying to be like Daddy.'

"After a few moments of indecision, I asked Rachel, 'What's wrong with trying to be like Dad?'

"When I finished telling the story, I looked at my father and added, 'That's what I've always tried to do.'"

When your children love you with all their hearts, they will follow your best examples and learn all that you have to offer them.[113]

For I have given you an example,
that ye should do as I have done to you.
JOHN 13:15 KJV

A man once gave his little boy a baseball and a baseball bat, but he never pitched the ball to his son or showed him how to swing the bat. He gave his boy a toy gun, but he never showed him how to play "cop" with it, instead of robber. The man gave his son a pocket-knife, but he never showed him how to use it properly.

> *Children as a rule do not want to be indulged. They want to be responsible.*

He gave his boy a BB gun, but he never took him to a firing range to show him how to use it safely.

The man was astonished the day two policemen came to his door with a tale about his son and others in the neighborhood who had formed a malicious gang. "Not my son," he said. "I've never taught him violence."

"Perhaps not," the policeman answered. "But in the shed that the boys were using for their headquarters, we found clubs, guns, and knives. Maybe you didn't teach your son how *not* to be violent."

Children need parents to show them what to expect in life, how to embrace life, and how to live life to its fullest.[114]

*Even a child is known by his actions,
by whether his conduct is pure and right.*
PROVERBS 20:11

> *To understand your parents' love, you must raise children yourself.*

The following was adapted from a selection by John C. Maxwell called *Getting to Know God with Your Children:*

"God was a part of our everyday existence, as regular a part of conversation as sports or school or doing the dishes. So was prayer. My mother prayed daily for us before we left for school. In fact, I can remember when her prayers for me to resist temptation flashed through my head and stopped me from cheating on a test that I hadn't studied for. We should never underestimate the power of our example on our children. We teach what we know, but we reproduce what we are. Much of what we do today was modeled for us by our parents."

John's wife, Margaret, compared people to kernels of popcorn. "God has a plan for each of us to become a very special person," she writes in the book, "but we haven't become that special person yet. We're like these kernels of popcorn. They can change, but they can't pop all by themselves—they need help from the power of the stove or the microwave oven. We're just like that. We need God's power to become the person He wants us to be."

Don't underestimate how much influence you have with your children on a daily basis![115]

For you know that we dealt with each of you as a father deals with his own children, encouraging, comforting and urging you to live lives worthy of God.
1 THESSALONIANS 2:11-12

Each Day

Each day, I promise myself not to try to solve all my life problems at once—nor shall I expect you to do so.

Starting each day, I shall remember to communicate my joy as well as my despair, so that we can know each other better.

Starting each day, I shall remind myself to really listen to you and to try to hear

> *The joys of parents are secret, and so are their griefs and fears.*

your point of view and to discover the least-threatening way of giving you mine, remembering that we are both growing and changing in a hundred different ways.

Starting each day, I shall try to be more aware of the beautiful things in our world—I'll look at the flowers, I'll look at the birds, I'll look at the children, I'll feel the cool breezes, I'll eat good food—and I'll share these things with you.

Starting each day, I shall remind myself to reach out and touch you, gently, with my words, my eyes, and with my fingers, because I don't want to miss feeling you.

You know, I'm really convinced that if you were to define love, the only word big enough to engulf it all would be "life."

Love is life in all its aspects.[116]

May your fountain be blessed, and may you rejoice in the wife of your youth.
PROVERBS 5:18

> # Children need love,
> ## especially when they
> ### do not deserve it.

Humorist Erma Bombeck once wrote: "Every mother has a favorite child. She cannot help it. She is only human. I have mine—the child for whom I feel a special closeness, with whom I share a love that no one else could possibly understand. My favorite child is the one who was too sick to eat ice cream at his birthday party . . . who had measles at Christmas . . . who wore leg braces to bed because he toed in . . . who had a fever in the middle of the night, the asthma attack, the child in my arms at the emergency ward.

"My favorite child is the one who messed up the piano recital, misspelled *committee* in a spelling bee, ran the wrong way with a football, and had his bike stolen because he was careless.

"My favorite child was selfish, immature, bad-tempered, and self-centered. He was vulnerable, lonely, unsure of what he was doing in the world—and quite wonderful.

"All mothers have their favorite child. It is always the same one: the one who needs you at the moment. Who needs you for whatever reason—to cling to, to shout at, to hurt, to hug, to flatter, to reverse charges to, to unload on—but mostly just to be there."

Make your children feel special by always being there for them, just as our heavenly Father is always there for us.[117]

Be ye therefore merciful,
as your Father also is merciful.
LUKE 6:36 KJV

"When we first moved to northern Idaho, our front yard consisted of nothing but weeds," Pastor Stephen Bly writes in *How to Be a Good Dad*. "Sooner or later, we had to tackle the yard. Mike, at fifteen, seemed a likely prospect to handle the job. But about five minutes after starting, he came back into the house. 'I need some gloves,' he reported. . . . He spent twenty minutes looking for gloves. After a brief time back in the yard, he returned again. 'I've got to have some music. . . .' He spent fifteen minutes setting up his portable stereo. . . . Ten minutes later I saw him again. 'It's hot out there. I've got to have a drink.' Finally, I thought I heard him chopping. But not for long . . . 'Hey, Dad,' he said, 'you know what we need? If we had one of those electric weed whips. . . .'

> *Work is the meat of life, pleasure the dessert.*

"'Mike!' I began in my best drill sergeant's voice, 'I don't care if it takes you all day, all week, or all month. You and that hoe are going to chop down every weed. Then you're going to rake them and carry them off. Now, stop stalling.'"

Children who are taught to stick with the job until it's finished have learned a skill that will be in great demand, both in school and when they enter the work force.[118]

The sleep of a labouring man is sweet.
ECCLESIASTES 5:12 KJV

241

> Children seldom misquote you.
> In fact, they usually repeat word for
> word what you shouldn't have said.

"You're talking so loud I can't hear you," is a popular phrase. Good advice about "taming the tongue" has been offered by essentially every culture, tribe, and race! The following poem reveals some of that advice:

"The boneless tongue,
    so small and weak,

Can crush and kill,"
    declares the Greek.

"The tongue destroys
    a greater horde,"

The Turk asserts,
    "than does the sword."

The Persian proverb wisely saith,

"A lengthy tongue—an early death!"

Or sometimes takes this form instead,

"Don't let your tongue
    cut off your head."

"The tongue can speak
    a word whose speed,"

Say the Chinese, "outstrips the steed."

The Arab sages said in part,

"The tongue's great storehouse
    is the heart."

From Hebrew was the maxim sprung,

"Thy feet should slip,
    but ne'er the tongue."

The sacred writer crowns the whole,

"Who keeps the tongue
    doth keep his soul."

The answer to many of the problems we experience may very well lie in the tongue. Teach your children that they don't have to tell all that they know.[119]

In everything set them an example by doing what is good. In your teaching show integrity, seriousness and soundness of speech.
TITUS 2:7-8

During the Depression, many families could scarcely afford the bare essentials, much less Christmas presents. "But, I'll tell you what we can do," a father said to his six-year-old son, Pete. "We can use our imaginations and make pictures of the presents we would like to give each other."

> *Success is getting what you want; happiness is wanting what you get.*

For the next few days, each member of the family worked secretly, but joyfully. On Christmas morning huddled around a tree decorated with a few pitiful decorations, the family exchanged the presents they had created. Daddy got a shiny black limousine and a red motor boat. Mom received a diamond bracelet and a new hat. Little Pete had fun opening his gifts: a drawing of a swimming pool and pictures of toys cut from magazines.

Then it was Pete's turn to give his presents. With great delight, he handed his parents a brightly colored crayon drawing of three people—man, woman, and little boy. They had their arms around one another and under the picture was one word: "US." Even though other Christmases were far more prosperous for this family, no Christmas in the family's memory stands out as more precious than the year they discovered their greatest gift was each other.[120]

A merry heart maketh a cheerful countenance.
PROVERBS 15:13 KJV

245

> *Look for a lovely thing
> and you will find it.*

A legal secretary was disgusted and depressed as she left from work one rainy afternoon.

She had been hearing about other people's problems all day long, which wasn't new and usually didn't bother her, but this day had also been filled with injustice. A client came in crying because her estranged husband had taken their young children and wouldn't let her see them. Another client who had worked hard all his life and was now disabled had been denied Social Security disability benefits. His case would have to be appealed.

As she stepped out of the building, the rain added more gloom to her dreary outlook. She walked to her car still thinking about all the injustices of the world. As she drove through town, she silently pleaded with God to do something to cheer her up. Just then, she stopped at a red light. There in the sky beyond the traffic was a bright, exhilarating rainbow that brought tears of relief and joy to her eyes. God did care! The rainbow reminded her of God's compassion for His people and the promise that Jesus will return someday.

When the injustices of life and other problems get you down, look for the rainbow![121]

Be content with such things as ye have.
HEBREWS 13:5 KJV

When the great golfer Babe Didrikson Zaharias was dying of cancer, her husband, George Zaharias, came to her bedside. Although he desired to be strong for her sake, he found he was unable to control his emotions and began to cry. Babe said to him gently, "Now honey, don't take on so. While I've been in the hospital, I

> *First keep peace within yourself, then you can also bring peace to others.*

have learned one thing. A moment of happiness is a lifetime, and I have had a lot of happiness."

Happiness does not come wrapped in brightly colored packages as a gift given to us by others. Happiness comes when we uncover the gifts that lie within us and begin to use them to please God and bless others.

Happiness flows from within. It is found in the moments of life we label as quality rather than quantity. George Bernard Shaw once wrote, "This is the true joy in life: Being used for a purpose recognized by yourself as a mighty one . . . being a force of nature instead of a feverish, selfish, little clod of ailments and grievances, complaining that the world will not devote itself to making you happy." Become at peace with yourself, and others will follow.[122]

I have stilled and quieted my soul.
PSALMS 131:2

249

> *The most beautiful action in the world is to love. The second most beautiful is to give.*

The story is told of two men who worshipped God in the same church. One of the men was poor, barely able to earn enough to support himself and his family even though he desired to work and serve God. The other man was rich, mainly because of an inheritance that he had wisely invested and managed. The rich man determined that he would help the poor man, giving gifts to him through a friend so as to remain anonymous. With the first gift he gave, he wrote a little note: "This is yours. Use it wisely. There is more to follow."

A few weeks later, he sent a second gift with the same message. Over the weeks and months that followed, the rich man noticed that his money didn't seem to be the least bit decreased. He also noticed that the poor man was still struggling; he seemed plagued by problems in his health and misfortunes that were not always of his own doing. The rich man increased his giving, always with a note that said, "More to follow."

For many individuals, life is a constant struggle just to provide the basic necessities. For others, life provides more materially than they could ever possibly spend in their lifetimes. Ask yourself how you can be a blessing to someone today.[123]

The light in the eyes [of him whose heart is joyful] rejoices the hearts of others.
PROVERBS 15:30 AMP

During the Civil War, a Quaker son left home against his father's wishes and enlisted on the side of the North. Time passed and no word was heard from him. One night the father had a dream that his son was in great need.

The next morning, the father left the farm and made

> *Blessed is the man who keeps in touch with his child's heart.*

his way by horse-drawn buggy to the battlefield. In asking about his son, he learned that the troops had been under heavy fire earlier in the day and many had fallen wounded. The father asked for permission to try to find his son. The commander wearily granted it.

The father searched late into the afternoon. When it was dark, he lit a lantern and went from person to person, letting the light fall across the faces of the wounded young men. As he stumbled among the bodies, he began calling loudly, "Jonathan Smythe, thy father seeketh after thee."

Diligently, he kept at his search until, finally, he heard a very faint, barely audible reply, "Father, over here." And then, "I knew you would come."

Can your children count on you to find them and come to their assistance when they are in distress?[124]

A patient man has great understanding.
PROVERBS 14:29

253

Direct your efforts more to preparing youth for the path and less preparing the path for youth.

DeAnna and Ronda Miller grew up in a small town in Georgia, a close-knit black community where poverty was the standard. Their mother, Lucille Miller, worked two and sometimes three jobs to make ends meet. Although their home had no indoor plumbing and circumstances were harsh, DeAnna became salutatorian of her class. Ronda became one of the few black valedictorians in the history of Ludowici High School in Long County, Georgia.

DeAnna entered Benedict College in South Carolina as a pre-med biology major; Ronda majored in psychology at Spelman College in Atlanta. Behind their accomplishments were their faith, hard work, and a deep love for their mother, who stood by them and instilled in them excellence of character and a love of learning.

DeAnna and Ronda were blessed with friends and family who cared about them. But even more so, they were taught the tools to overcome adversity and the value of working for their achievements.[125]

*Now devote your heart and soul
to seeking the LORD your God.*
1 CHRONICLES 22:19

General Douglas MacArthur once said, "By profession I am a soldier, and take pride in that fact. But I am more proud, infinitely more, to be a father. A soldier destroys in order to build; a father only builds, never destroys. The one has the potentialities of death, the other embodies creation and life. While the hordes of death· are mighty, the battalions of life are mightier still. It is my hope that my son, when I am gone, will remember me not from the battles, but in the home, repeating with him our simple daily prayer, 'Our Father, who art in Heaven.'"

> *Anything large enough for a wish to light upon is large enough to hang a prayer on.*

These words by General MacArthur reflect his priorities in life. A parent who gives his children the example of prayer provides for them a foundation upon which to base all their decisions.

Prayer is not difficult. What is difficult is living without God's presence beside you daily, both during the good times and the bad. Talk to Him throughout the day just as you would a good friend, which indeed He is. God doesn't ask for big words or rehearsed speeches; He wants to hear what is in your heart.[126]

By day the LORD directs his love, at night his song is with me—a prayer to the God of my life.
PSALMS 42:8

The following true story happened several years ago in the Paris opera house. A celebrated singer had been contracted to sing, and ticket sales were booming. The night of the concert found the house packed and every ticket sold. A feeling of anticipation and excitement was in the air as the house director took the stage and said, "Ladies and gentlemen, thank you for your enthusiastic support. I am afraid that due to illness the man whom you've all come to hear will not be performing tonight. However, we have found a suitable substitute we hope will provide you with comparable entertainment." The crowd groaned in disappointment and failed to hear the announcer mention the stand-in's name. The environment turned from excitement to frustration.

The stand-in artist gave the performance everything he had. When he had finished, there was nothing but an uneasy silence. No one applauded. Suddenly, from the balcony, a little boy stood up and shouted, "Daddy, I think you are wonderful!" The crowd broke into booming applause.

This little boy loved his father and showed everyone attending the performance just how much. Live your life with enthusiasm, and your children will develop an enthusiasm for life.[127]

Shout with joy to God, all the earth! Sing the glory of his name; make his praise glorious!
PSALMS 66:1-2

Janet was apprehensive about the dinner party that she and her husband were hosting that evening. It was their first time to have guests for dinner since their son, James, was born. Adding to Janet's distress was the fact that one of their guests was her husband's new supervisor.

Always laugh when you can. It is cheap medicine.

Sensing the tension in his parents, the baby became cranky and fretful, which only increased Janet's frustration with the situation. In an attempt to comfort little James, Janet picked him up, raised him high over her head, and kissed his bare tummy. To her amazement, he smiled and giggled— the first genuine laughter she had heard from her young son.

In that moment, the evening took on an entirely new tone. Janet became more relaxed, and baby James calmed down and went off to sleep. The dinner party was enjoyed by everyone, including the new supervisor.

The laughter of a child can change the mood of a parent's entire day. So can laughter shared between adults, or a smile prompted by the memory of a funny event.

Find a reason to laugh and watch the tension melt away. Laughter is good for the soul and the body.[128]

Be joyful always.
1 THESSALONIANS 5:16

> *You don't learn to praise in a day,
> especially since you may have
> been complaining for years!*

Charles Wesley wrote one of the great hymns of the church on May 21, 1749, the eleventh anniversary of his conversion to Christianity. The German Moravians had a great influence on Charles after his conversion. They were Christians who loved to sing and emphasized a personal conversion experience.

Peter Bohler, a Moravian leader, once said, "Had I a thousand tongues, I would praise Christ Jesus with all of them." Charles took that statement and built a hymn around it, not only to celebrate the date of his own conversion, but also to encourage others to give ongoing praise throughout their lives for their salvation and deliverance.

He wrote:

"O for a thousand tongues to sing my great Redeemer's praise,

The glories of my God and King, the triumphs of His grace!

Jesus! the name that calms our fears, that bids our sorrows cease,

'Tis music in the sinners' ears, 'tis life, and health, and peace.

He breaks the power of canceled sin, He sets the prisoner free;

His blood can make the foulest clean; His blood availed for me. . . ."

Glorifying God through music and song is a wonderful way to express your salvation through Jesus Christ.[129]

My heart is steadfast, O God; I will sing and make music with all my soul.
PSALMS 108:1

Hugs

It's wondrous what a hug can do. A hug can cheer you when you're blue.

A hug can say, "I love you so," or "I hate to see you go."

A hug is "Welcome back again," and "great to see you! Where've you been?"

> *It's never too late to have a happy childhood.*

A hug can soothe a small child's pain, and bring a rainbow after rain.

A hug, there's just no doubt about it— We scarcely could survive without it!

A hug delights and warms and charms. It must be why God gave us arms.

Hugs are great for fathers and mothers, sweet for sisters, swell for brothers.

And chances are your favorite aunts love them more than potted plants.

Kittens crave, puppies love them; heads of state are not above them.

A hug can break the language barrier, and make travel so much merrier.

No need to fret about your store of 'em; the more you give, the more there's more of 'em.

So stretch those arms without delay and give someone a hug today!

The fortunate ones grew up with an abundance of hugs during their childhood years. Those who didn't now have the opportunity to practice for themselves. Open your arms and experience happiness![130]

A merry heart doeth good like a medicine:
but a broken spirit drieth the bones.
PROVERBS 17:22 KJV

> *The only power that can
> resist the power of fear
> is the power of love.*

While driving along the freeway, the adults in the front seat of the car were horrified by the sound of a car door opening, the whistle of wind, and the unforgettable thud of a child hitting the ground. The three-year-old girl riding in the back seat of the car had fallen out and was tumbling along the highway. The driver screeched to a stop, then raced back to her daughter. To her surprise, the mother found that all the traffic had stopped just a few feet away from her little girl. Her child had not been hit!

A truck driver took the girl to a nearby hospital where the doctors rushed her into the emergency room. They soon came back with the good news that, other than a few scrapes and bruises, the little girl was fine.

As the mother ran to her daughter, the little girl opened her eyes and said, "Mommy, you know I wasn't afraid. While I was lying on the road waiting for you to get back to me, I looked up and right there I imagined Jesus holding back the traffic with His arms out."

The power of love conquers fear![131]

When I am afraid, I will trust in you.
PSALMS 56:3

Tom Bodett once shared an incident about his little boy, who was not quite two years of age at the time. His son's vocabulary consisted of only a few words: more, no, hello, bye-bye, Momma, and Daddy. These words made up his standard conversation, except for one word. His least-used word was "wow," which he uttered only when something truly impressed him.

> *The soul is healed by being with children.*

One night Tom, his wife, and his little boy stayed at a friend's house. He and his wife set up a crib in the guest bedroom next to their bed. Tom said he slept well, but he woke up too early and couldn't get back to sleep. Lying awake in the unfamiliar house gave him the opportunity to hear his son wake up for the first time. He heard his child stir. The little boy rolled over, opened his eyes, and said, "Wow!"

What a wonderful way to wake up in the morning! It's probably as close to contentment as a person could ever get. See the world through your children's eyes and reawaken your wonderment at God's creation.[132]

Sing to him a new song; play
skillfully, and shout for joy.
PSALMS 33:3

269

> *Kind words can be short and easy to speak, but their echoes are truly endless.*

One day the Reverend John Newton called upon a Christian family who had suffered the loss of all they possessed in a devastating fire. He greeted the wife and mother of the family by saying, "I give you joy."

The woman seemed surprised at his words—almost offended—and replied, "What! Joy that all my property is consumed?"

"Oh, no," Newton answered, "but joy that you have so much property that fire cannot touch."

His words reminded her of the true riches of her life, those things that she valued beyond measure: Her husband, whom she loved very much; her children, the light of her life; the good health that they all possessed; their joy in each other and their faith in God; the love of an extended family and friends; and their prayers for a future together.

None of these riches can be bought, bargained, or appraised. They come from within the heart, and in the joy and peace of mind that comes from our belief in Jesus Christ. Surely it was His hand that brought her family safely through their ordeal.

What simple words of encouragement can you give to your children?[133]

A word fitly spoken is like apples of gold in pictures of silver.
PROVERBS 25:11 KJV

One day a fisherman was lying on a beautiful beach with his fishing pole propped up in the sand. About that time, a businessman came walking down the beach.

"You aren't going to catch many fish that way," said the businessman to the fisherman. "You should be working rather than lying on the beach!"

The fisherman looked up at the businessman, smiled, and replied, "And what will my reward be?"

> *The best thing about the future is that it comes only one day at a time.*

"Well, you can get bigger nets and catch more fish!" was the businessman's answer.

"And then what will my reward be?" asked the fisherman.

The businessman replied, "You will make money."

"And then what will my reward be?" asked the fisherman again.

The businessman was getting angry. "Don't you understand? You can build up a fleet of fishing boats."

Again the fisherman asked, "And then what will my reward be?"

The businessman shouted at the fisherman, "Don't you understand that you can become so rich that you will never have to work for your living again! You can spend all the rest of your days sitting on this beach, looking at the sunset."

The fisherman, still smiling, looked up and said, "And what do you think I'm doing right now?"

Look to the future, but enjoy the beauty of each precious day.[134]

When my spirit grows faint within me,
it is you who know my way.
PSALMS 142:3

> *Faith will lead you where you cannot walk. Reason has never been a mountain climber.*

The great English poet, Samuel Taylor Coleridge, was once talking with a man who told him that he did not believe in giving children any religious training whatsoever. His philosophy was that the child's mind should not be biased in any direction, but when he came to years of discretion he should be permitted to choose his religious opinions for himself. Mr. Coleridge said nothing, but after a while he asked his visitor if he would like to see his garden. The man replied that he would, and Coleridge took him out into the garden where only weeds were growing. The man looked at Coleridge in surprise, and said, "Why, this is not a garden! There are nothing but weeds here!"

"Well, you see," answered Coleridge, "I did not wish to infringe upon the liberty of the garden in any way. I was just giving the garden a chance to express itself and to choose its own production."

Are you allowing your children to make all the decisions about their education, or will you build a foundation in them on which to base their faith?[135]

My son, give me thine heart.
PROVERBS 23:26 KJV

Acceptance by the peer group is extremely important to a teenager. Some adolescents will exhibit extreme behavior to become one of the group. They are willing to alienate parents and family just to be accepted. One father faced this type of situation and reacted to it in the following way:

> *If you judge people, you have no time to love them.*

"A banker was appalled when his awkward teenage son began wearing ragged clothing and an earring in his ear. His first impulse was to demand that his son 'shape up and clean up.' But before he said anything, he thought, *My son must feel that he isn't a part of the school crowd. He's dressing this way to feel accepted. Rather than work on his dress, I need to work on his self-esteem.*

"A few weeks later, the father invited his son to go with him to his annual banker's club banquet. The two had a great time. Even though the son sported an orange streak in his hair, he wore a suit to the event and behaved superbly, recalling the names of his father's friends and confidently conversing with them. He had responded to the unspoken message of his father's invitation: 'Son, I'm proud of you.'"

This father knew that his son needed loving help and guidance—not judgment. Look at your child's heart before you criticize his hair.[136]

Judge not, and ye shall not be judged:
condemn not, and ye shall not be condemned.
LUKE 6:37 KJV

> *Nobody spots a phony quicker than a child.*

One Sunday morning, a minister announced to his congregation that the topic for the next Sunday's sermon would be "integrity." In preparation, he asked them to study the wisdom of Solomon found in Proverbs 32.

The minister began the service the next Sunday by asking the congregation how many had read the assigned scripture. Several hands were raised when the question was asked.

"Just as I thought," said the minister, "there is no 32nd chapter in the book of Proverbs. Thereby, the need for this sermon on honesty."

One of the first lessons parents usually teach their preschoolers is: "Thou shalt not tell a lie." We expect our children to tell us the truth whatever the circumstances. In return we should model the same behavior. Too many times parents excuse their behavior by making excuses: "It's just a little white lie; they wouldn't understand."

Children understand when someone isn't being truthful with them. It's not necessary to give them a long explanation and go into all the details that they probably wouldn't be able to understand, but it is possible to give them an age-appropriate and truthful answer.[137]

Provide things honest in the sight of all men.
ROMANS 12:17 KJV

One stormy day, a coast guard ship was ordered to the rescue of a liner wrecked off the coast of New England. An old and tried seaman was in charge, but the members of the crew were for the most part young and untested men. When one of them compre-hended the situation, he turned chalky-faced to the captain and said, "Sir, the wind is offshore; the tide is running out. We can go out, but against this wind and tide we cannot come back."

> *Courage is fear that has said its prayers.*

The grim old captain faced the young man and said, "Launch the boat; we go out."

"But, sir!" protested the young man.

"We don't have to come back, replied the captain."

This old captain knew that without coast guard help the crew of the wrecked liner would most likely be lost to the impelling force of the sea. He made the courageous decision to launch his boat even though he knew that he might be sacrificing his own crew in so doing.

Do you have the courage to make the right decision in every situation? Only with God's help can we hope to be brave enough![138]

Let your light shine before men,
that they may see your good deeds
and praise your Father in heaven.
MATTHEW 5:16

281

> *Trouble knocked at the door but, hearing a laugh within, hurried away.*

Charles Swindoll wrote in *Growing Strong in the Seasons of Life:*

"Tonight was fun 'n games night around the supper table in our house. It was wild. First of all, one of the kids snickered during the prayer (which isn't that unusual) and that tipped the first domino. Then a humorous incident from school was shared and the event (as well as how it was told) triggered havoc around the table. That was the beginning of twenty to thirty minutes of the loudest, silliest, most enjoyable laughter you can imagine. At one point, I watched my oldest literally fall off his chair in hysterics, my youngest doubled over in his chair as his face wound up in his plate with corn chips stuck to his cheeks . . . and my two girls leaning back, lost and preoccupied in the most beautiful and beneficial therapy God ever granted humanity: laughter.

"What is so amazing is that everything seemed far less serious and heavy. Irritability and impatience were ignored like unwanted guests. For example during the meal, little Chuck spilled his drink twice . . . and even that brought the house down."

Laughter is truly a gift from God! Make time for it in your daily life.[139]

If God be for us, who can be against us?
ROMANS 8:31 KJV

In 1863 a creative engineer named John Roebling was inspired by an idea for the construction of the Brooklyn Bridge. However, bridge-building experts throughout the world told him to forget it; it could not be done.

Roebling convinced his son, Washington, who was also an engineer, that the bridge could be built. The two of them developed the concepts of how it could be accomplished and how the obstacles could be overcome.

> *Somebody is always doing what somebody else said couldn't be done.*

The project had only been underway a few months when a tragic accident on the site took the life of John Roebling and severely injured his son. Washington was left with permanent brain damage, unable to talk or walk. Everyone felt that the project would have to be scrapped.

However, Washington's mind was as sharp as ever, and he still had a burning desire to complete the bridge. He developed a code for communication. All he could move was one finger, so he tapped out the code on his wife's arm. He communicated to her what to tell the engineers who were building the bridge. This lasted for thirteen years until the spectacular bridge was completed.

There is always a way with God's help.[140]

Anything is possible if you have faith.
MARK 9:23 TLB

> *A day hemmed in prayer*
> *is less likely to unravel.*

Spiritual giants in every age have agreed about prayer: more is better. The founder of Methodism, John Wesley, spent one to two hours a day in private communication with God. The great Scottish preacher, John Welch, regularly prayed eight to ten hours a day, and then often awoke in the middle of the night to continue his conversation with the Lord. Both Martin Luther and Bishop Francis Asbury believed two hours of prayer a day was a minimum.

These were not men who had nothing else to do. All advocated that a person combine prayer with work, including praying as one works.

Today many parents lead such busy lives that they often think they have no time for

286

prayer on behalf of their families. Yet the most powerful thing a parent can do is pray. As you drive to work, walk from place to place, or do mundane chores, talk to God at length about each child. Thank God for your children. Listen for His advice.

The change in your children and your relationship with them is likely to be remarkable, even miraculous! And remember to spend some of that precious time in prayer *with* your children.[141]

We always thank God for all of you,
mentioning you in our prayers.
1 THESSALONIANS 1:2

Throughout Brenda's early childhood, school meant failure and frustration for her. She had a reading disability. While her older brother was a straight "A" student, Brenda barely managed a "C" average. Every one of her teachers for the first five grades came to the same conclusion: She was a lazy daydreamer who lacked the ability to do any better. Brenda lived up to those expectations for years.

> *All kids are gifted; some just open their packages earlier than others.*

Then her sixth grade teacher changed things. Mrs. Barnes pulled Brenda aside on the first day of school and said, "I've heard a lot about you, and I don't believe a word of it."

She showed Brenda a copy of an aptitude test that she had taken the year before. "You have so much ability! I know you have a learning problem, but I'm going to find a way to help you."

During the year, Mrs. Barnes worked hard at finding ways to help Brenda feel good about herself. She taught Brenda to compare herself with what she could become, and not with her own past or that of others.

Due to the influence of this special teacher, Brenda graduated with honors. She not only learned to read but found the tools to become more than she ever dreamed possible. Not all flowers blossom at the same time, and neither do children.[142]

Don't show favoritism.
JAMES 2:1

> *The more we depend on God, the more dependable we find He is.*

There is a story about an English steamer that was wrecked on a rocky coast many years ago. Twelve women set out into the dark stormy waters in a lifeboat, and the turbulent sea immediately carried them away from the wreckage. Having no oars, they were at the mercy of the wind and the waves. They spent a fearful night being tossed about by the raging storm.

They probably would have lost all hope if it had not been for the spiritual stamina of one woman who was well known for her work in sacred performances. Calmly, she prayed aloud for divine protection. Then urging her companions to put their trust in the Lord, she encouraged them by singing hymns of comfort.

Throughout the dark hours, her voice rang out across the water. Early the next morning, a small craft came searching for survivors. The man at the helm would have missed the women in the fog if he had not heard a woman singing the selection from *Elijah*. "Oh, rest in the Lord, wait patiently for Him!" Steering in the direction of her strong voice, he soon spotted the drifting lifeboat. While many others were lost that night, these trusting few were rescued.

Teach your children to trust in God![143]

Faith is being sure of what we hope for and certain of what we do not see.
HEBREWS 11:1

When Linda was an overweight girl growing up in the shadow of older siblings, her grandmother held her, cuddled her, and showered her with an abundance of praise. In her grandma's presence, Linda was always "her girl." No matter what she did or how she looked, Grandma was steadfast in her opinion that deep inside Linda was special.

> *If you have love in your heart, you always have something to give.*

Now that Linda is an adult, her grandmother continues to pray for and encourage her. She's shown Linda her need for Christ through her own consistent relationship with Him. Linda has seen in her grandmother how God works through His children to reach others and achieve His will. One of the most important messages God sent to Linda by way of her grandmother was that He loves her. She's not just part of a church congregation or a family member—she's someone with whom God wants to have a one-on-one relationship.

Linda's grandma accomplished all this by loving her granddaughter unconditionally and openly sharing her faith with her throughout the years. She knew the value of love in the development of a child's personality, self-confidence, pride, and faith. Love given is love shared.[144]

May the Lord make your love increase and overflow for each other and for everyone else.
1 THESSALONIANS 3:12

> *Each day of our lives we make deposits in the memory banks of our children.*

For years Jeff had been driving past an old house outside of town, gawking at the remains of a grand wraparound front porch. He finally stopped.

It reminded him of his grandmother's wide, big-pillared porch set among the trees in Wisconsin. In those days, a front porch was a central part of the house and its daily routine. It was a command post for parents and grandparents who kept an eye on the children playing in the neighborhood.

But grandmother's porch was more than that. On rainy days, the porch was a playground, limited only by imagination. On hot summer afternoons, the porch sat pooled in the coolest shade. On hot nights, there'd be bursts of laughter and the slap of cards as aunts and uncles played. Each Sunday, Grandpa would sit alone in his rocker reading the newspaper.

Not many of us experience those things much anymore. Air-conditioning has moved most of us indoors to sit in front of the television, or to the mall or the movie theater.

Life moved slower back then, and maybe it wasn't such a bad idea, taking the time to porch-sit and relax from the day's activities. Try turning off the television to make a memory with your child.[145]

The just man walketh in his integrity:
his children are blessed after him.
PROVERBS 20:7 KJV

Sparky never had much going for him. He failed every subject in the eighth grade and several in high school. He was awkward, both physically and socially. Sparky was a teenager who never quite fit in anywhere. He did make the golf team, but then lost the most important match of the season. During his high school years, he never once asked a girl out on a date.

> *Our greatest glory is not in never failing but in rising up every time we fail.*

The most important thing in Sparky's life was his drawing. He was proud of his artwork, even though no one else appreciated it. He submitted cartoons to the editors of his high school yearbook, but they were rejected. He sent samples of his artwork to the Walt Disney Studios. Once again, his work was rejected.

Sparky refused to quit! He continued to have confidence in his ability to create art. After being turned down by Walt Disney, he decided to write his own autobiography in cartoons. The character he created was Charlie Brown, who became famous worldwide. Sparky was Charles Schulz, creator of the "Peanuts" comic strip. What a loss it would have been if Sparky had quit after his first rejection and not tried again to bring his work to the public eye![146]

Blessed is the man who perseveres under trial, because when he has stood the test, he will receive the crown of life.
JAMES 1:12

> *We worry about what a child will be tomorrow, yet we forget that he is someone today.*

Many children are growing up today in single parent homes and need role models to help them determine their place in society. Adults are volunteering to fulfill this role.

One such example of these volunteers is Ken Canfield who became a "Big Brother" to a boy named Brian. Brian's parents were divorced, and his mother asked if Ken could spend some time with her son. Ken and Brian spent many Saturdays together with Brian watching and listening closely to everything Ken said. They never did anything extravagant—just hung out together. One experience helped Ken to realize that God's plan is to provide a male role model for the fatherless. Ken wrote the following short letter to his "little brother":

"Dear Brian, I'm looking forward to getting together again with you this Saturday. I've enjoyed our time together, and I just want you to know that you're a great guy to be around. Your Big Brother, Ken."

The next time Ken visited Brian, he saw his letter proudly displayed on Brian's wall surrounded by posters of sports heroes.

Live one day at a time with your child. The little things you do together will have a major impact on the future.[147]

Don't be anxious about tomorrow.
God will take care of your tomorrow too.
Live one day at a time.
MATTHEW 6:34 TLB

Just for Today

"Just for today, decide to be happy, to live with what is yours—your family, your business, your job, your luck. If you can't have what you like, maybe you can like what you have.

"Just for today, be as kind, cheerful, agreeable, responsive, caring, and understanding as you can. Be your best, dress your best, talk softly, and look for the bright side of things. Praise people for what they do and do not criticize them for what they cannot do. If a person does something stupid, forgive and forget. After all, it's just for one day. Who knows, it might turn out to be a nice day!

"Just for today, try to live through this one day only and not tackle all your

> *Cleaning your house while your kids are still growing is like shoveling the walk before it stops snowing.*

problems at once. You can do something for twelve hours that would appall you if you felt that you had to keep it up for a lifetime.

"Just for today, have a quiet half-hour all by yourself and relax.

"Just for today, be unafraid. Especially do not be afraid to enjoy what is beautiful and to believe that as you give to the world, so the world will give to you."

Happiness comes from the contentment gained by living life one day at a time.[148]

For I have learned, in whatsoever state I am, therewith to be content. . . . I can do all things through Christ which strengtheneth me.
PHILIPPIANS 4:11,13 KJV

301

> *God loves each of us as if
> there were only one of us.*

The majority of mothers have a vast capacity for love. Christian Author John Killinger wrote, "I believe in the love of all mothers, and its importance in the lives of the children they bear. It is stronger than steel, softer than down, and more resilient than a green sapling on the hillside. It closes wounds, melts disappointments, and enables the weakest child to stand tall and straight in the fields of adversity. I believe that this love, even at its best, is only a shadow of the love of God. . . . And I believe that one of the most beautiful sights in the world is a mother who lets this greater love flow through her to her child, blessing the world with the tenderness of her touch and the tears of her joy."

This beautiful selection expresses so clearly the special love that a mother has for her children. That love never wavers. It stays constant throughout the bad times and the good.[149]

The LORD *is my light and my salvation.*
PSALMS 27:1

There is a humorous story about an elderly man who vowed that he would never ride in an airplane. He always said that if he couldn't get there by car, he just wouldn't go! One day, however, an emergency arose and it was necessary for him to get to a faraway city in a short amount of time. Of course, the fastest way to get there was by air. With trepidation he purchased a ticket and made his first trip in an airplane.

> *Worry: the interest paid by those who borrow trouble.*

Knowing of his reluctance to fly, his relatives met him at the airport. They asked him how he enjoyed the flight. He responded, "Oh, it was all right, I guess. But I'll tell you one thing. I never let my *full weight* down on the seat."

Unlike the elderly man in the airplane, God wants us to cast the full weight of our cares upon Him and leave them there. Do this with your daily concerns and problems of parenthood, as well as all the future decisions you'll make about your children. It will make the journey so much more enjoyable![150]

Cast your cares on the LORD and he will sustain you; he will never let the righteous fall.
PSALMS 55:22

> *Out of the mouths of babes come words we shouldn't have said in the first place.*

A small boy's parents were excited about a special gift they had purchased for their son. They had bought him a compact disc/cassette tape player. They were sure he had no idea what was in this package under the Christmas tree.

A couple of days before Christmas, they realized that they did not have any CDs for the player. They took the package from beneath the tree, went on one final shopping trip to buy CDs, and rewrapped the player with the CDs inside.

The son noticed that the package was gone and asked his parents about it. His dad came up with the perfect alibi. "You see, son, Santa wanted to look at your present. After he looked at it, he wrapped it up again and gave it back to us while we were out shopping."

Later that night, the parents noticed that their son was kneeling beside his bed saying his prayers. They heard him say, "God, You know I already prayed to you once tonight, but I have one more thing to say. I don't know why Dad blamed Santa for swiping my CD player, but I just want to thank You for getting Dad to bring it back."[151]

For out of the abundance of
the heart the mouth speaketh.
MATTHEW 12:34 KJV

Harold Reynolds, ESPN baseball analyst and one-time all-star second baseman for the Seattle Mariners, wrote:

"When I was growing up in Corvallis, Oregon, there was an NBA player named Gus Williams. Gus tied his shoes in back instead of in front like normal. I thought that was so cool.

> *No gift to your mother can ever equal her gift to you—life.*

So I started tying my shoes in the back. I wanted to be like Gus. He wore number 10; I wore number 10. He wore one wristband; I wore one wristband.

One day I was lying in bed and my stomach was killing me. I noticed that it wasn't my sports hero, Gus Willliams, who came to my room to take care of me. It was my mother.

That's when I began to understand the difference between heroes and role models.

I stopped looking at athletic accomplishments to determine who I wanted to pattern my life after. Instead, I tried to emulate people with strong character who were doing things of lasting value."

Most individuals learn this truth at some point in their lifetimes. For their sakes, one hopes they learn it as children. Others become aware of this truth as adolescents; others when they attain adulthood. The saddest ones are those who never learn the value of character.

Live your life in such a way that it will bring joy to your mother's heart.[152]

May your father and mother be glad:
may she who gave you birth rejoice!
PROVERBS 23:25

> *Being considerate of others will take your children further in life than any college degree.*

"A smile costs nothing but gives much. It enriches those who receive without making poorer those who give. It takes but a moment, but the memory of it sometimes lasts forever. None is so rich or mighty that he can get along without it and none is so poor that he cannot be made rich by it. A smile creates happiness in the home, fosters good will in business, and is the countersign of friendship. It brings rest to the weary, cheer to the discouraged, sunshine to the sad, and is nature's best antidote for trouble. Yet it cannot be bought, begged, borrowed, or stolen, for it is something that is of no value to anyone until it is given away. Some people are too tired to give you a smile. Give them one of yours, as none needs a smile so much as he who has no more to give."

—Anonymous

This anonymous writer has given us a recipe for success in life. Teach your children how to smile.[153]

A kind man benefits himself.
PROVERBS 11:17

One spring afternoon, Ben Stein, and his young son, Tommy, were wandering around the little town of Oxford, Maryland. They passed by the Academy House owned by the family of his high-school Latin teacher. Ben told Tommy, "She was a great teacher. She used to make us dress in togas to recite the Catilinarian Orations."

> *The joy that you give to others is the joy that comes back to you.*

After Ben told his son about Cicero, Catiline, and ancient Rome, Tommy emerged from his hotel bedroom wrapped in a sheet. "Like you, Daddy, a long time ago," he said, as Ben looked out the window so Tommy wouldn't see him crying with happiness.

The next day, Ben showed his son the route he used to take across Sligo Creek on a footbridge. He told Tommy about getting into a fistfight with another boy on the bridge.

"I bet you killed him, huh, Daddy," said Tommy.

"I doubt it; I don't think either of us landed a punch."

"But you're so strong!"

You're the only one on earth who thinks so! Ben laughed to himself. He patted Tommy's towhead and thanked God for his son.

What a wonderful experience to revisit the past through your child's eyes! You may be surprised to find out how much fun it is to share the memories of your childhood.[154]

A happy heart makes the face cheerful.
PROVERBS 15:13

Acknowledgments

The publisher would like to honor and acknowledge the following people for the quotes used in this book:

Mario Cuomo (6), Robert Gardner (8), Dr. Henker (10), C. Everett Koop (12), Michael Levine (14), Johann Wolfgang von Goethe (16), Winston Churchill (18), Wilferd A. Peterson (20), Harry Edwards (22), Oliver Wendell Holmes (24), Albert Einstein (26), Lady Bird Johnson (28), Zig Zigler (30), Joseph Joebert (32), Mary Mason (34), Charles Swindoll (38,136,294), Josh Billings (42), John Mason Brown (44), Oliver Goldsmith (48), Benjamin Franklin (50,174,228,282), Samuel Johnson (54,64), Thomas Fuller, M.D. (56), Gloria Gaither (58), Elbert Hubbard (60), David Jeremiah (62), Gordon MacDonald (66), Charles Spurgeon (68,76), Dan Quayle (70), Paul L. Lewis (72), Saint Francis Xavier (78), William J. Bennett (80), James Baldwin (82), Paul Tillich (84), Hodding Carter (86), Welsh Proverb (90), Sydney J. Harris (92,176), Sir Henry Taylor (94), Dwight Lyman Moody (96), Lord Byron (98,260), Sir Thomas Fuller (100), Ethel Barrymore (104), Peter Ustinov (106), Eleanor Roosevelt (110), Walter M. Schirra Sr. (112), John Lubbock (114), Thornton Wilder (116), William Makepeace Thackeray (122), Arnold Glasgow (124), Meng-Tzu (126), Henry Ward Beecher (128,168,216), Austin O'Malley (130), Abbe Dimnet (132), Theodore M. Hesburgh (138), Will Rogers (140), Benjamin Disraeli (144), William James (148), Robert C. Alberts (152), Elizabeth Stone (156), Rose Fitzgerald (162), Mother Teresa (164,270,276), Erma Bombeck (166), Wilhelm Busch (170), Ellen Key (172), Norman Vincent Peale (173), Dr. Judith Kariansky (178), George Herbert (180), Franklin P. Jones (182), Jean Jacques Rousseau (184), Erwin W. Lutzer (186,262), Chinese proverb (188), Kahlil Gibran (190), Henry Wadsworth Longfellow (192), Paul Tournier (194), Danish Proverb (198), Bertha Munro (206), William Butler Yeats (208), Henry Drummond (212), Søren Aabye Kierkegaard (214), Denis Diderot (218), Frank Clark (220), Thomas Jefferson (224), Peter Marshall (226), Thomas Carlyle (230), Hannah Lees (232), Francis Bacon (236), Oswald Chambers (238,256), B. C. Forbes (240), Sara Teasdale (246), Thomas à Kempis (248), Bertha Von Suttner (250), Benjamin Barr Lindsey (254), George MacDonald (256), Norman Vincent Peale (258), Tom Robbins (264), Alan Stewart Paton (266), Fyodor Dostoyevski (268), Abraham Lincoln (272), E. W. Kenyon (274), Mary MacCracken (278), Dorothy Bernard (280), Michael Carr (288), Cliff Richards (290), Ralph Waldo Emerson (296), Stacia Tauscher (298), Phyllis Diller (300), Saint Augustine of Hippo (302), George W. Lyon (304), Marian Wright Edelman (310), John Greenleaf Whittier (312).

Endnotes

1. Story adapted from Roy B. Zuck, *The Speaker's Quote Book*, Grand Rapids, Michigan, Kregel Publications, 1997, p.165.

2. Adapted from Roy B. Zuck, *The Speaker's Quote Book*, Grand Rapids, Michigan, Kregel Publications, 1997, p. 82.

3. Drawn from Kathy Collard Miller and D. Larry Miller, *God's Vitamin C for the Spirit*, Lancaster, Pennsylvania, Starburst Publishers, 1996, p. 64.

4. Edited from Jack Canfield, Mark Hansen, Hanock McCarty, Meladee McCarty, *A 4th Course of Chicken Soup for the Soul*, Deerfield Beach, Florida, Health Communications, Inc., 1997, pp. 133,134.

5. Found in Michael Hodgin, *1001 Humorous Illustrations for Public Speaking*, Grand Rapids, Michigan, Zondervan Publishing House, 1994, p. 151, #371.

6. Information found in Roy B. Zuck, *The Speaker's Quote Book*, Grand Rapids, Michigan, Kregel Publications, 1997, p. 262.

7. Edited from Edward K. Rowell, *Fresh Illustrations for Preaching and Teaching*, Grand Rapids, Michigan, Baker Books, 1997, p. 24.

8. Drawn from W. B. Freeman, *God's Little Lessons on Life for Mom*, Tulsa, Oklahoma, Honor Books, 1999, p. 51.

9. Information drawn from *Top 100 Inspirational Anecdotes and Wisdom* (part 3), found online @www.bizmove.com/inspiration, 1999, p. 9.

10. From Roy B. Zuck, *The Speaker's Quote Book*, Grand Rapids, Michigan, Kregel Publications, 1997, p. 147.

11. Information drawn from *Top 100 Inspirational Anecdotes and Wisdom* (part 1), found online @www.bizmove.com/inspiration, 1999, p. 6.

12. Information drawn from *Top 100 Inspirational Anecdotes and Wisdom* (part 5), found online @www.bizmove.com/inspiration, 1999, p. 7.

13. Edited from Craig Larson, *Choice Contemporary Stories and Illustrations for Preachers, Teachers, and Writers*, Grand Rapids, Michigan, Baker Books, 1998, p. 34.

14. Used from George Sweeting, *Who Said That*, Chicago, Illinois, Moody Press, 1995, p. 184.

15. Adapted from Roy B. Zuck, *The Speaker's Quote Book*, Grand Rapids, Michigan, Kregel Publications, 1997, p. 137.

16. Drawn from Dean Merrill, *Focus on the Family* magazine, 1996, found online @www.focusonthefamily, 1999, p. 2.

17. Story adapted from Craig Larson, *Choice Contemporary Stories and Illustrations for Preachers, Teachers, and Writers*, Grand Rapids, Michigan, Baker Books, 1998, p. 85.

18. Found in W. B. Freeman, *God's Little Lessons on Life for Mom*, Tulsa, Oklahoma, Honor Books, 1999, p. 17.

19. Drawn from *God's Little Devotional Book for Dads*, Tulsa, Oklahoma, Honor Books, 1995, p. 159.

20. Found online by Philippe, *Just for Parents*, @http://members.xoom.com/XMCM/BouBou/pr/parents8.htm, 1999, p. 8.

21. Edited from Roy B. Zuck, *The Speaker's Quote Book*, Grand Rapids, Michigan, Kregel Publications, 1997, pp. 234,236.

22. Information found online, *Top 100 Inspirational Anecdotes and Wisdom* (part 4), @www.bizmove.com/inspiration, 1999, p. 2.

23. Story adapted from *God's Little Devotional Book for Dads*, Tulsa, Oklahoma, Honor Books, 1995, p. 49.

24. From Kathy Collard Miller and D. Larry Miller, *God's Vitamin C for the Spirit*, Lancaster, Pennsylvania, Starburst Publishers, 1996, p. 192.

25. Drawn from *God's Little Devotional Book for Dads*, Tulsa, Oklahoma, Honor Books, 1995, p. 343.

26. Information adapted from John Maxwell, Teach Your Children Well, *Focus on the Family* magazine, 1996, found online @www.focusonthefamily, 1999, p. 1.

27. Based upon information Roy B. Zuck, *The Speaker's Quote Book*, Grand Rapids, Michigan, Kregel Publications, 1997, p. 163.

28. Edited from Jacob Braude, *Braudes Treasury of Wit & Humor for All Occasions*, Paramus, New Jersey, Prentice Hall, 1991, p. 139.

29. Based upon anecdote from Craig Larson, *Choice Contemporary Stories and Illustrations for Preachers, Teachers, and Writers*, Grand Rapids, Michigan, Baker Books, 1998, p. 140.

30. From James S. Hewett, *Illustrations Unlimited*, Wheaton, Illinois, Tyndale House Publishers, 1988, p. 235.

31. Drawn from *God's Little Devotional Book for Dads*, Tulsa, Oklahoma, Honor Books, 1995, p. 83.

32. Story adapted from Kimberly Southall, *Grandpa's Legacy*, 1997, found online @www.nytimes/christian, 1999.

33. Found in Kathy Collard Miller and D. Larry Miller, *God's Vitamin C for the Spirit*, Lancaster, Pennsylvania, Starburst Publishers, 1996, p. 29.

34. Adapted from *God's Little Devotional Book for Dads*, Tulsa, Oklahoma, Honor Books, 1995, p. 93.

35. Drawn from *God's Little Devotional Book for Dads*, Tulsa, Oklahoma, Honor Books, 1995, p. 27.

36. Anecdote drawn from *God's Little Devotional Book for Dads*, Tulsa, Oklahoma, Honor Books, p. 139.

37. Found in Herbert Prochnow, *Treasury of Inspiration*, Grand Rapids, Michigan, Baker Book House, 1958, pp. 66,67.

38. Edited from Herbert Prochnow, *Treasury of Inspiration*, Grand Rapids, Michigan, Baker Book House, 1958, pp. 79,80.

39. Story adapted from *God's Little Devotional Book for Dads*, Tulsa, Oklahoma, Honor Books, 1995, p. 9.

40. Adapted from *Encyclopedia of 7700 Illustrations*, Paul Lee Tan, editor, Dallas, Texas, Bible Communications, 1979, pp. 501-502.

41. Drawn from *Top 100 Inspirational Anecdotes and Wisdom* (part 5), found online @www.bizmove.com/inspiration, 1999, p. 1.

42. Excerpt found *God's Little Devotional Book for Dads*, Tulsa, Oklahoma, Honor Books, 1995, p. 33.

43. Found in Herbert Prochnow, *Treasury of Inspiration*, Grand Rapids, Michigan, Baker Book House, 1958, p. 49.

44. Drawn from compiler W. B. Freeman, *God's Little Lessons on Life for Mom*, Tulsa, Oklahoma, Honor Books, 1999, p. 45.

45. Found online @focusonthefamily/parentsplace, 1999, p. 3.

46. Drawn from Herbert Prochnow, *Treasury of Inspiration*, Grand Rapids, Michigan, Baker Book House, 1958, p. 21.

47. Edited from Claire Cloninger, *A Childlike Heart, Women's Devotional Bible #2*, NIV, Grand Rapids, Michigan, Zondervan Publishing House, 1995, p. 519.

48. Found in *Top 100 Inspirational Anecdotes and Wisdom* (part 2), online @www.bizmove.com/inspiration, 1999, p. 1.

49. Edited from *God's Little Devotional Book for Dads*, Tulsa, Oklahoma, Honor Books, 1995, p. 173.

50. Adapted from George Sweeting, *Who Said That*, Chicago, Illinois, Moody Press, 1995, pp. 247,248.

51. Story adapted from *God's Little Devotional Book for Dads*, Tulsa, Oklahoma, Honor Books, 1995, p. 101.

52. Based upon anecdote George Sweeting, *Who Said That*, Chicago, Illinois, Moody Press, 1995, p. 203.

53. Drawn from *Top 100 Inspirational Anecdotes and Wisdom* (part 2), found online @www.bizmove.com/inspiration, 1999, pp. 8-10.

54. Found in Paul Lee Tan, editor, *Encyclopedia of 7700 Illustrations*, Dallas, Texas, Bible Communications, 1979, p. 1008.

55. Information found in *Top 100 Inspirational Anecdotes and Wisdom* (part 4), found online @www.bizmove.com/inspiration, 1999, p. 2.

56. Drawn from *Top 100 Inspirational Anecdotes and Wisdom* (part 5), found online @www.bizmove.com/inspiration, 1999, p. 7.

57. Edited from article found online @www.christianity.net/tcw/8w5/8w5066.html, Sherrie Lathrop, *Today's Christian Woman*, Jackson, Washington, September/October 1998.

58. Found in *God's Little Devotional Book for Dads*, Tulsa, Oklahoma, Honor Books, 1995, p. 75.

59. Story found in Herbert Prochnow, *Treasury of Inspiration*, Grand Rapids, Michigan, Baker Book House, 1958, p. 20.

60. Found in Craig Larson, *Choice Contemporary Stories and Illustrations for Preachers, Teachers, and Writers*, Grand Rapids, Michigan, Baker Books, 1998, p. 47.

61. Edited from *Like a Child, Christian Fellowship Devotionals*, found online @www.cfdevotionals.org, August 5, 1999.

62. Found in *Top 100 Inspirational Anecdotes and Wisdom* (part 5), online @www.bizmove.com/inspiration, 1999, p. 7.

63. Edited from *Top 100 Inspirational Anecdotes and Wisdom* (part 4), found online @www.bizmove.com/inspiration, 1999, p. 5

64. Drawn from Parents Place, *Focus on the Family*, found online @www.focusonthefamily, 1999, p. 3.

65. Story adapted from compiler, W. B. Freeman, *God's Little Lessons on Life for Mom*, Tulsa, Oklahoma, Honor Books, 1999, p. 83.

66. Adapted from *God's Little Devotional Book for Dads*, Tulsa, Oklahoma, Honor Books, 1995, p. 69.

67. Found in Craig Larson, *Choice Contemporary Stories and Illustrations for Preachers, Teachers, and Writers*, Grand Rapids, Michigan, Baker Books, 1998, p. 29.

68. Edited from George Sweeting, *Who Said That*, Chicago, Illinois, Moody Press, 1995, p. 45.

69. Drawn from compiler J. Dargatz, *God Will Make a Way*, Tulsa, Oklahoma, Albury Publishing, 1999, pp. 156,157.

70. Adapted from Edward K. Rowell, editor, *Quotes & Idea Starters for Preaching & Teaching*, Grand Rapids, Michigan, Baker Books, 1996, pp. 9,18,19.

71. Quote by Roy B. Zuck, *The Speaker's Quote Book*, Grand Rapids, Michigan, Kregel Publications, 1997, p. 148.

72. Found in Top 100 *Inspirational Anecdotes and Wisdom* (part 5), online @www.bizmove.com/inspiration, 1999, pp. 2,3.

73. Adapted from Dr. Scudders *Daily Reflections*, found online @aol.com, 1999.

74. Edited from George Sweeting, *Who Said That*, Chicago, Illinois, Moody Press, 1995, p. 337.

75. Drawn from *God's Little Devotional Book*, Tulsa, Oklahoma, Honor Books, 1998, p. 127.

76. Found in *Top 100 Inspirational Anecdotes and Wisdom* (part 4), found online @www.bizmove.com/inspiration, 1999, pp. 4,5.

77. Found in *Top 100 Inspirational Anecdotes and Wisdom* (part 5), found online @www.bizmove.com/inspiration, 1999, pp. 5,6.

78. Adapted from *God's Little Devotional Book for Dads*, Tulsa, Oklahoma, Honor Books, 1995, p. 175.

79. Drawn from Karen Mains, *Welcome, Child, to My Home, Women's Devotional Bible #2*, NIV, Grand Rapids, Michigan, Zondervan Publishing House, 1995, p. 1083.

80. Found in Roy B. Zuck, *The Speaker's Quote Book*, Grand Rapids, Michigan, Kregel Publications, 1997, p. 237.

81. Adapted from George Sweeting, *Who Said That*, Chicago, Illinois, Moody Press, 1995, p. 194.

82. Edited from Roy B. Zuck, *The Speaker's Quote Book*, Grand Rapids, Michigan, Kregel Publications, 1997, p. 263.

83. Drawn from Craig Larson, *Choice Contemporary Stories and Illustrations for Preachers, Teachers, and Writers*, Grand Rapids, Michigan, Baker Books, 1998, p. 33.

84. Adapted from *1100 Illustrations from the Writings of D. L. Moody*, John W. Reed, editor, Grand Rapids, Michigan, Baker Book House, 1996, p. 18.

85. Found in *God's Little Devotional Book for Dads*, Tulsa, Oklahoma, Honor Books, 1995, p. 207.

86. Drawn from Linda Jewel, N.M., *It's Better to Give, Christianity Today*, Inc., Today's Christian Woman, September/October 1998, volume 20, #5, p. 66.

87. Edited from *God's Little Devotional Book for Dads*, Tulsa, Oklahoma, Honor Books, 1955, p. 245.

88. Found in *God's Little Devotional Book for Dads*, Tulsa, Oklahoma, Honor Books, 1955, p. 11.

89. Drawn from *Words that Hurt or Words that Heal*, Larry Davies, Sowing Seeds Ministry, found online 8-19-99.

90. Edited from George Sweeting, *Who Said That*, Chicago, Illinois, Moody Press, 1995, p. 371.

91. Adapted from W. B. Freeman, compiler, *God's Little Lessons on Life for Mom*, Tulsa, Oklahoma, Honor Books, 1999, p. 47.

92. Story found in Roy B. Zuck, *The Speaker's Quote Book*, Grand Rapids, Michigan, Kregel Publications, 1997, p. 49.

93. Drawn from Jack Canfield, Mark Hansen, Hanock McCarty, Meladee McCarty, *A 4th Course of Chicken Soup for the Soul*, Deerfield Beach, Florida, Health Communications, Inc., 1997, pp. 239,240.

94. Edited from Craig Larson, *Choice Contemporary Stories and Illustrations for Preachers, Teachers, and Writers*, Grand Rapids, Michigan, Baker Books, 1998, p. 13.

95. Found in Roy B. Zuck, *The Speaker's Quote Book*, Grand Rapids, Michigan, Kregel Publications, 1997, p. 239.

96. Drawn from Cyndi Webb, *If I Had My Child to Raise Over Again*, Just for Parents, found online @http://members.xoom.com/XMCM/BouBou/pr/parents3.htm, 12-9-99.

97. Story from *God's Little Devotional Book for Dads*, Tulsa, Oklahoma, Honor Books, 1995, p. 105.

98. Story adapted from *God's Little Devotional Book for Dads*, Tulsa, Oklahoma, Honor Books, 1995, p. 177.

99. Drawn from Roy B. Zuck, *The Speaker's Quote Book*, Grand Rapids, Michigan, Kregel Publications, 1997, p. 52.

100. Drawn from *God's Little Devotional Book for Dads*, Tulsa, Oklahoma, Honor Books, 1995, p. 119.

101. Found in John Croyle, *Parent's Place, Love Unconditionally*, online @focusonthefamily, 1999, p. 1,2.

102. Found in A Special Teacher, *Top 100 Inspirational Anecdotes and Wisdom* (part 4), online @www.bizmove.com/inspiration, 1999, pp. 3,4.

103. Edited from Todd Outcalt, *Seeing Is Believing,* Nashville, Tennessee, Abingdon Press, 1999, p. 40.

104. Adapted from *Afterhours Inspirational Stories,* found online Inspirational Stories: June 1998.

105. Drawn from *God's Little Devotional Book for Dads,* Tulsa, Oklahoma, Honor Books, 1995, p. 59.

106. Found in Craig Larson, editor, *Illustrations for Preaching and Teaching,* Grand Rapids, Michigan, Baker Book House, 1993, p. 281.

107. Based upon Herbert Prochnow, *Treasury of Inspiration,* Grand Rapids, Michigan, Baker Book House, 1958, pp. 58,59.

108. Edited from Craig Larson, *Choice Contemporary Stories and Illustrations for Preachers, Teachers, and Writers,* Grand Rapids, Michigan, Baker Books, 1998, p. 175.

109. Found in *God's Little Devotional Book for Dads,* Tulsa, Oklahoma, Honor Books, 1995, p. 205.

110. Adapted from *Top 100 Inspirational Anecdotes and Wisdom* (part 3), found online @www.bizmove.com/inspiration, 1999, p. 2.

111. Based upon *God's Little Devotional Book for Dads,* Tulsa, Oklahoma, Honor Books, 1995, p. 29.

112. Drawn from *God's Little Devotional Book for Dads,* Tulsa, Oklahoma, Honor Books, 1995, p. 55.

113. Adapted from Craig Larson, *Choice Contemporary Stories and Illustrations for Preachers, Teachers, and Writers,* Grand Rapids, Michigan, Baker Books, 1998, p. 136.

114. Edited from *God's Little Devotional Book for Dads,* Tulsa, Oklahoma, Honor Books, p. 35.

115. Found in John Maxwell, *Getting to Know God with Your Children,* Focus on the Family magazine, 1995, online @www.focusonthefamily, 1999.

116. Information found in *Top 100 Inspirational Anecdotes and Wisdom* (part 3), online @www.bizmove.com/inspiration, 1999, p. 4.

117. Story from *God's Little Devotional Book for Moms,* Tulsa, Oklahoma, Honor Books, p. 165.

118. Edited from *God's Little Devotional Book for Dads,* Tulsa, Oklahoma, Honor Books, 1995, p. 183.

119. Story from *God's Little Devotional Book for Dads,* Tulsa, Oklahoma, Honor Books, 1995, p. 25.

120. Adapted from compiler W. B. Freeman, *God's Little Lessons on Life for Mom,* Tulsa, Oklahoma, Honor Books, 1999, p. 63.

121. Drawn from *Look for the Rainbow,* Christian internet site, www.nytimes, 1999.

122. Edited from compiler W. B. Freeman, *God's Little Lessons on Life for Mom,* Tulsa, Oklahoma, Honor Books, 1999, p. 95.

123. Story edited from *1100 Illustrations from the Writings of D. L. Moody,* John Reed, editor, Grand Rapids, Michigan, Baker Book House, 1996, p. 124.

124. Found in *God's Little Devotional Book for Dads,* Tulsa, Oklahoma, Honor Books, 1995, p. 43.

125. Adapted from Todd Outcalt, *Seeing Is Believing,* Nashville, Tennessee, Abingdon Press, 1999, p. 19.

126. Edited from Herbert Prochnow, *Treasury of Inspiration,* Grand Rapids, Michigan, Baker Book House, 1958, p. 86.

127. Drawn from *Top 100 Inspirational Anecdotes and Wisdom* (part 5), found online @www.bizmove.com/inspiration, 1999, p. 1.

128. Based upon compiler W. B. Freeman, *God's Little Lessons on Life for Mom,* Tulsa, Oklahoma, Honor Books, 1999, p. 9.

129. Drawn from *The One Year Book of Hymns,* Robert K. Brown and Mark R. Norton, editors, Wheaton, Illinois, Tyndale House Publishers, 1995, July 8 entry.

130. Found in Roy B. Zuck, *The Speaker's Quote Book,* Grand Rapids, Michigan, Kregel Publications, 1997, pp. 236,237.

131. Edited from compiler W. B. Freeman, *God's Little Lessons on Life for Mom,* Tulsa, Oklahoma, Honor Books, 1999, p. 163.

132. Based upon Tom E. Bodett, Mouths of Babes, condensed from Small Comforts as printed in *Readers Digest,* June 1991, found online @www.readersdigest, 1995.

133. From *1100 Illustrations from the Writings of D. L. Moody,* John Reed, editor, Grand Rapids, Michigan Baker Book House, 1996, p. 247.

134. Found online, *What Will My Reward Be?,* @http://members.xoom.com/XMCM/BouBou/stories.htm,1999, pp. 9,10.

135. Adapted from Roy B. Zuck, *The Speaker's Quote Book,* Grand Rapids, Michigan, Kregel Publications, 1997, pp. 51,52.

136. Drawn from compiler W. B. Freeman, *God's Little Lessons on Life for Mom,* Tulsa, Oklahoma, Honor Books, 1999, p. 187.

137. Edited from Jacob Braude, *Braudes Treasury of Wit & Humor for all Occasions, Paramus,* New Jersey, Prentice Hall, 1991, p. 94.

138. Found in Herbert Prochnow, *Treasury of Inspiration,* Grand Rapids, Michigan, Baker Book House, 1998, p. 10.

139. Edited from compiler W. B. Freeman, *God's Little Lessons on Life for Mom*, Tulsa, Oklahoma, Honor Books, 1999, p. 201.

140. Drawn from *Top 100 Inspirational Anecdotes and Wisdom* (part 3), found online @www.bizmove.com/inspiration, 1999, p. 1.

141. Story found in *God's Little Devotional Book for Dads*, Tulsa, Oklahoma, Honor Books, 1995, p. 57.

142. Found online at *Christianity Today, Inc.*, Today's Christian Woman magazine, September/October 1998, Vol. 29, No. 5, p. 66.

143. Story edited from compiler W. B. Freeman, *Sunset with God*, Tulsa, Oklahoma, Honor Books, 1999, p. 138,139.

144. Found online at *Christianity Today, Inc.*, Today's Christian Woman magazine, God Loves You and So Do I, September/October 1998, Vol. 29.

145. Drawn from Jeff Rennicke, Wisconsin Trails, This Place of Summer Dreams, *Reader's Digest*, June 1997, online @www.readersdigest.

146. Edited from compiler W. B. Freeman, *God's Little Lessons on Life for Mom*, Tulsa, Oklahoma, Honor Books, 1999, p. 170.

147. Found in Craig Larson, *Choice Contemporary Stories and Illustrations for Preachers, Teachers, and Writers*, Grand Rapids, Michigan, Baker Books, 1998, p. 231.

148. Drawn from Just for Today, *Top 100 Inspirational Anecdotes and Wisdom* (part 2), found online @www.bizmove.com/inspiration, 1999, pp. 3,4.

149. Edited from Edward K. Rowell, editor, *Quotes & Idea Starters for Preaching & Teaching*, Grand Rapids, Michigan, Baker Books, 1996, p. 116.

150. Drawn from compiler W. B. Freeman, *Sunset with God*, Tulsa, Oklahoma, Honor Books, 1999, pp. 14,15.

151. Found in Michael Hodgin, *1001 More Humorous Illustrations for Public Speaking*, Grand Rapids, Michigan, Zondervan Publishing House, 1998, p. 40.

152. Edited from Craig Larson, *Choice Contemporary Stories and Illustrations for Preachers, Teachers, and Writers*, Grand Rapids, Michigan, Baker Books, 1998, p. 232.

153. Found in George Sweeting, *Who Said That*, Chicago, Illinois, Moody Press, 1955, p. 255.

154. Edited from Benjamin J. Stein, My No. 1 Priority, Washingtonian, *Reader's Digest*, November 1996, found online @www.readersdigest, 1999.

Additional copies of this book and other titles in the *God's Little Devotional Book* series are available from your local bookstore.
Also look for our
Special Gift Editions in this series.

God's Little Devotional Book
God's Little Devotional Book for Women
God's Little Devotional Book for Men
God's Little Devotional Book for Moms
God's Little Devotional Book for Dads
God's Little Devotional Book for Students
God's Little Devotional Book for Graduates
God's Little Devotional Book for Teachers
God's Little Devotional Book for Teens

If you have enjoyed this book,
or if it has impacted your life,
we would like to hear from you.
Please contact us at:

Honor Books
Department E
P.O. Box 55388
Tulsa, Oklahoma 74155

or by e-mail: info@honorbooks.com